OUT OF THE DREAMING DARK

Poems by F. Mary Callan

Illustrations by Joy Simpson

Stairwell Books

www.stairwellbooks.co.uk

FOREWORD

In 1992 I was counselled into writing.
Two years later I discovered I could write rhyming verse, and spent an ecstatic morning writing my first sonnets.
What to do with this new skill? What theme would encompass my varied interests: my fascination with science, the beauty of the natural world, human beings and their many talents?
I was sick of miserable and brutal poetry.
I wanted to restore beauty and joy, without being dishonest about our real world.
I chose the Bible's seven days of creation as my theme, although each 'Day' may have lasted millions/billions of years.
The result is **Out of the Dreaming Dark.**

Some of the early poems flowed easily, some were dug and cemented. Day Four was a real struggle. With experience the poems became simpler, but I have learnt that readers are as varied as writers: one person's favourite will be the one another hates. The bricks and cement sometimes refuse to be smoothed. A few certainly deserve to be binned, but contain valid ideas, or revisit images and vocabulary that pull the sequence together. All my poems benefit by being spoken aloud. I hope you enjoy them all.

I am thrilled with the illustrations by my artist daughter, **Joy Simpson.**
The flower photos are my own.

APPRECIATION for OUT OF THE DREAMING DARK

As exciting as a novel

Gorgeous illustrations

"A tour de force! . . celebrating joy, beauty and growth" (John Gilham)

A wide range of voices here, some very grave and grand, some rough or cheeky, and plenty of fun.

THE POETRY IS SOMETIMES FEEBLE,
THE IDEAS NEVER.

At last, this lovely poet offers her work to the world's audience.

THE ILLUSTRATIONS ALONE WOULD MAKE THIS PRICELESS.

~ DEDICATION ~

CREDO ***God for all Times and Seasons***

You are the God of sun and stars and moon,
Seven days' variety: light and shade;
Earth and water; fire's glow, wind's tune;
Eggs and turtles and giant ferns; all made,

All master-minded, all adapted,
Each to its place, and fitted to survive:
Polar bears in snow; trails where the moose led;
Owls in winter trees: warmth alive!

Snakes for the desert, lizards in cracks,
Speed for open plains: gnu and gazelle;
Songbirds for woodlands, fox leaving tracks,
Eagles for uplands: heath and harebell.

And us, in the heart's varied landscape:
Stormy seas, or the waves' gentle lap,
Home-hearth's glow or the blasting volcano,
Fumbling mist, where we can't see a scrap!

Through all we have shepherd and teacher,
To lift and support and urge on:
God, who challenges and feeds every creature,
And, in all our trials, loves each one.

~~~ CONTENTS ~~~

Page Title

Credo *God for all times and seasons*

~~~ Day I ~~~

2 Creation
3 Sparking Off
4 Creation II - The Mirror
5 New film of a lightning storm, 1994

~~~ Day 2 ~~~

8 The Vault and The Abyss

~~~ Day 3 ~~~

10 The Separation of Land and Water
11 Earth's Secrets
12 Variety
12 Greenery
13 Sea Power
14 Reprise : the English Lake District
14 Out of the Darkness (Coal)
15 The Blueprint
15 Fruit
16 Snowdrops
16 Winter Wallflower
17 Cyclamens
17 Pulmonaria
18 Larkspur & Nigella
18 Stray violets
19 First Blossom
19 Alpine flowers
20 Spring promise
21 Tulips I
21 Tulips II
22 Iris
23 Obedient Servants
24 Coffee-break on the Allotment
24 Yellow and Blue
25 Scarlet Poppy
26 Three Roses
26 Autumn Roses
27 Day's Eyes
27 Planting Schemes
28 Daffodil – Patience
29 Wild Mullein
29 Last Poppy
30 The First Chinese Lantern
30 Chinese Lanterns
31 Nasturtiums
31 Cosmos
32 Passion Flower
32 Sloes
33 Oak Leaves
33 Autumn Leaves
34 Aloe Flower
34 Negative Perfect
36 Bananas
37 Gourds & Pumpkins
37 Fungi

~~~ Day 4 ~~~

40 Into Focus: the Sun
41 Lunar Exploration
42 Wifely Advice: the moon speaks
43 Day & Night
44 Designer lamps
45 Winter
45 Spring
46 Late Spring
47 Summer, 1950s
47 Mediterranean summer
48 Autumn
48 November poem

~~~ Day 5 ~~~

50 Limits
50 Coral Reef
50 Tidal Zone
51 Sea Monsters

52 Sea-Shore Shells
53 The Pearl
54 Feathers
54 Airborne !
54 High Hopes
56 Brooding
56 The Singing Garden
57 The Song
58 The Albino Pigeon
59 The Pigeons' Garland
59 Blackbirds
60 The Peacock's Praise
61 The Peacock's Family
61 Street Peacock
61 Albino Peacock
62 Ducks in the Orchard
62 Hornbills
63 Golden Pheasant
64 Magpies
64 Magpies at a Roadside Cafe
65 Ladybirds
65 Butterfly

~~~ **Day 6** ~~~

68 Land Animals
68 Quadrupeds
69 Caterpillar
69 Snakes
70 Kangaroos
71 Reaching
72 21stC Camel
72 Lizard
73 One Lonely Sheep
74 Motherhood
74 Kitten Love
75 Debutantes
75 Belonging
76 Garden Mysteries (Grey Squirrel)
76 Under the Larch Trees

~~~ **Day 6 - Humans** ~~~

78 Human Beings
78 Four Elements – the Baker
79 Four Elements – the Glass-Blower
80 Plato & Co.
81 Noah's Peacock
82 The Spark - Michelangelo's Adam
82 Benjamin Franklin : the Unknown
83 People of Prayer (Contemplatives)
84 Electricians
84 Pylons
85 Trees
85 The Plant Breeder
86 The Gardener
86 Tapestry
87 to Jane Asher
88 Office Birthday
89 to Alison Hargreaves, Mountaineer
90 The Prospector
91 The Cartographer
92 Between the Tides – the Fossil Hunter
93 Bob Geldof : Band-Aid, Live-Aid
94 Aid Worker ?
94 to Shakespeare - Thanks for 'Romeo & Juliet'
95 From Homer to Kipling - Making Sense
96 Poetry Slam
97 Cigarettes – ex-teacher to ex-student
98 The Physiotherapist
98 Roofer
99 Vendor's Corner
99 Vendor's Shuffle
100 Pub Bands
100 Recognition

~~~ **Day 7** ~~~

101 Consummation
102 Poet’s Last Word
~~~

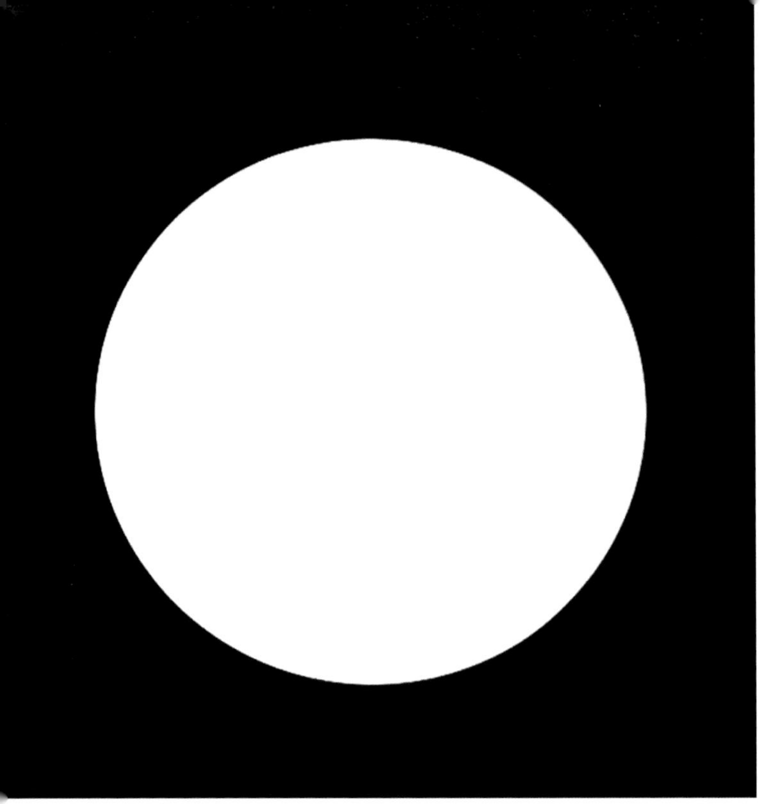

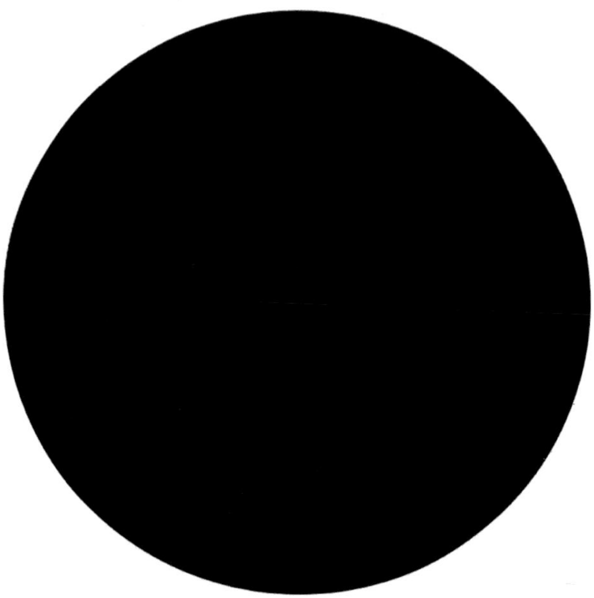

~~~ DAY I ~~~

Here begins the Bible account of the creation of the world, in the book of Genesis.
Day 1 is verses 1-5

It all started with God creating

the heavens and the earth.
The earth was shapeless and empty;

just bottomless darkness;

with God's Spirit brooding over it.

God said, "Let's have light,"

and light came into existence.

Light received God's approval.
God separated the light from the darkness.
God called the light "day."

His name for darkness was "night." Evening was followed by morning—

the first day was complete.

Genesis 1,1-5

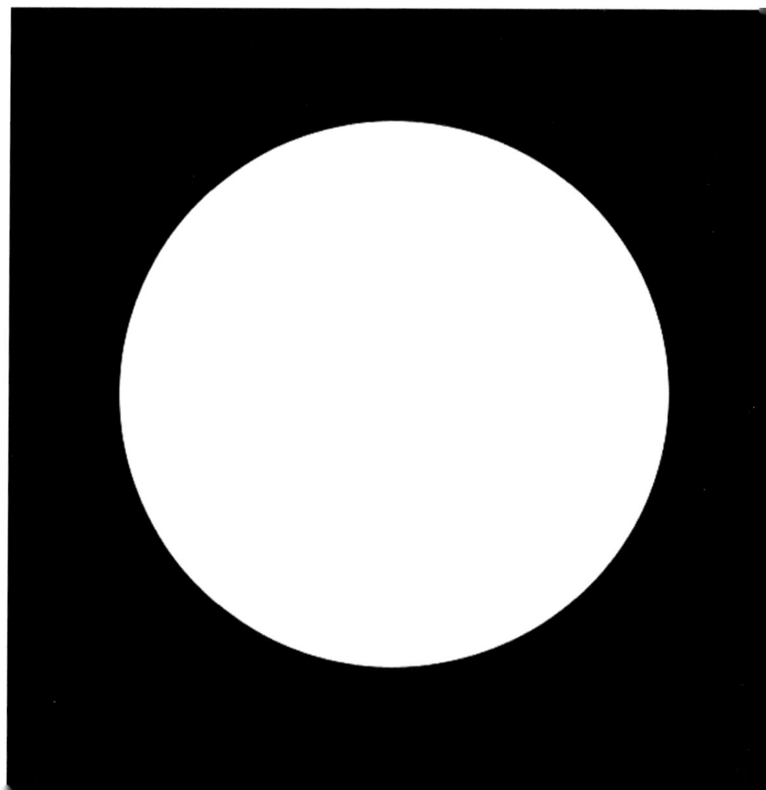

CREATION

Out of the dreaming dark, where *LOVE* and *LIFE*
Dance unhindered in the emptiness,
The give-and-take of *GODHEAD*, by its spark,
Causes creation: something out of nothingness.

BEING itself, *EXISTENCE* without constraint,
Confers existence on a world we can measure.
PEACE, uninhibited, ignites the faint
Pulse of a quark; the beginning of order; the pleasure

Of a universe forming; system in system evolving,
Looping spools of spheres, galaxies on their axes;
From atoms to deepest space, matter revolving,
Evolving, resolving, revealing its identities;

And by its ordered progress, bringing delight
To *BEING* itself, who summons it out of the night.

SPARKING OFF

As lonely as the only spark in space;
Unique and friendless: Why am I here?
Imprisoned in this vast and vacant place;
Echoing questions; shapeless, draining fear.

Ravenous emptiness laps at my door;
Empty greyness answers within.
The busy electron buzzes before,
Beside, around me, holding me in.

Anchorless, with nothing to do:
There is no *doing* yet, no-one to *do* it!
Just emptiness, the endless view
Into oblivion – mine! – No-one to know, I blew it!

Yet still, around, beside, buzzes the spark,
Pestering positron ringing me round,
Fencing me off from the hungry dark,
Rousing, focusing: dazzle and sound.

Why can't it fizzle out, extinct?
End its irritating presence?
Snuffed out, indistinct
From the nothing around me?
I sense
It slowing down, coming to terms
With my dejection, the meaninglessness.
It ticks at my own speed; affirms
My idleness and helplessness.

This dizzy spark is mine, to have and hold,
Defining me from the dark, giving me value:
Energy to fly free or bond; be bold,
Be active, or just admire the view.

Driven by this sizzle, or in the driving seat,
I shall exist for ever, playing many parts,
In space, or crowds, where many energies meet,
Driven and driving; now is where it starts!

Content to be, by being; my own spark
Looping around me, giving me room,
Defining my existence. Through the dark,
Working or playing, I'll use my zoom!

CREATION II - THE MIRROR

Love calls us out of nothing. In our darkness
Where we find only chaos, empty waste,
Love's light sees form, and licks us into wholeness,
Lighting up every contour. Sunlight traced

And caresses our emerging presence, precedes our progress
Like torches lighting our triumphal way
Teaching the path to the toddler; happy egress
To the outside world, urged by the beckoning day.

So love, the mirror, shows us a self unknown,
And loves us forth, into action, our truth to display,
Believing, first, in the mirror, at last, in ourselves.
Love's work is freely given. In debt to no-one
The beloved walks free, no shackling debts to pay,
Far from the mirror, giving love now, ourselves;

So love, bereft, yet other lives shall reach.
Love grows, as it gives, unending love to teach.

1994, NEW FILM OF A LIGHTNING STORM

Like silver snakes they danced in the crimson sky,
Shimmering and glowing, winding and weaving their light,
A ballet of flickering flashes; the human eye
Entranced by the sinuous chorus; electric delight:

The dance of the lightning, filmed far above the clouds,
Transmitted with all its mystery onto our screens;
Technology's magic, sharing out to the crowds
The secrets of science, fantastical fairy-tale scenes.

Like wisps from a witch's cauldron, this flickering brew
Entrances the seekers of knowledge, sets minds in a spin.
This blows the lid off their theories! All they knew
Is back into question. Which calculations will win

And capture these slithering flashes, as the magic of mind
Reached up beyond the clouds this new vision to find?

~~~ DAY 2 ~~~

And God said,
"Let there be an arch between the two lots of water to separate one lot of water from the other."

So God made the arch and separated the water under the arch from

the water above it.

So that was that sorted.

God called the arch "sky."
Evening was followed by morning—

the second day was complete.

Book of Genesis 1,6-8

VAULT & ABYSS

(Genesis 1, 6-8; Mt 27,46; Mk 15,34)

The vault above us, the abyss below;
An ordered firmament: the second day.
A child's-eye view. The primitive need to know
The framework of our lives won't totter and sway.

The arching sky, firm in its distant place,
The solid earth, unshaken under our feet,
Welcome the toddler's confidence. Protective space!
Explore and marvel and govern. Progress sweet.

WE have probed and questioned and shaken the foundations.
In this parentless world, we can pull the sky down on our heads.
The abyss of drugs and defeat issues devouring invitations.
Tossed among the flotsam and jetsam, what hope can we spread?

Anchor of the universe, where have you gone?
Will the God we have forsaken, reclaim his dying son?

~~~ DAY 3 ~~~

And God said,

"Let the water under the sky be collected to one place, and let dry ground appear."

And it happened.

God called the dry ground "land,"

and the collected waters he called "seas."
And God gave it His approval.

Then God said,
"Let the land grow vegetation:

seed-bearing plants and trees on the land
yielding fruit with seed in it,
according to their various species."

And that's what happened.

The land grew vegetation:

plants bearing seed according to their species
and trees yielding fruit with seed in it
according to their species.

And God gave it His approval.

Evening was followed by morning—

the third day was complete.

Book of Genesis 1,7-13

THE SEPARATION OF LAND & WATER

God's work is permanent. God's work is fruitful:
A partnership of contrasts: land and sea;
Solid and fluid; useful both, and beautiful;
Wet and dry; dull and reflecting; fixed and free.

Watch the waves crash against the rocks.
What power is there! Beauty! Majesty!
Trickling back, the foam combs the seaweed's locks,
Adapting to every crevice of its stubborn adversary.

The battle, sometimes gentle, sometimes violent,
Slowly eroding, slowly building up;
Sculptured coves and headlands, stern impediment,
Or soft sand, laid in layers, silting up.

The ever restless works on the ever still;
Impatience and patience, working God's will.

EARTH'S SECRETS

Grrr-ound, drry grr-rrr-ound, gritty and silent;
Sorted and separate from the foaming sea;
Hard-wearing, hard-bearing, solid and patient,
Waiting to be worked on, its secrets to free.

What history of torment and upheaval
Dull ground conceals, mute under our feet:
Extinct volcanoes, struggles primaeval,
Pressures and stresses where continents meet.

Wrinkled and twisted; buckle and fold;
Silt and shale, boulderclay, granite and marble;
Impossible pressures forge diamonds and gold,
Prepare coal, mystic opals, fossils to marvel;

Wealth in waiting, under the quiet earth,
Waiting for partnership, farmers and quarrymen,
Sculptors and architects; the slow birth
Of civilisation; miners and smiths and flint
marksmen.

Dinosaur fossils will lure the tapping prospector
To map and explore and theorise over earth's story;
The riches of partnership, raided and stripped from
the strata;
The challenge of guardianship, paying with graft for
the glory.

Till the sixth day, the secrets of earth can't be shown,
Underground archives till humans unearth the
unknown.

VARIETY

Infinitesimal nothings, charged with a value,
Swirling together, cooling, this pool of power;
Fusion and confusion, confrontation of energies,
Condensing, collapsing, reforming, sparking shower;

Earth swirls to a ball in its giddy corner:
Liquid squeezes from solid like whey out of curd;
And, curdling still, and boiling, hissing and seething,
Compounding and settling, steaming, everything blurred;

The pain of clinging to who one is,
Pressured by neighbours, tempted by emptiness;
Clinging to allies, changing valency,
Structuring, splitting, combining; sharing frequencies.

From core to crust, the struggle to accommodate,
Finding new strength, a richer structure:
Crystals and diamonds, opals or aggregate,
Iron and antimony form in the mixture.

Shrinking and cooling and settling at last;
Harder or purer, richer, more flexible,
Grown even more different, forged by its past,
Faithful, contented, enduring through trouble.

From simple sparks pressured unbearably tight
Worlds of variety spin day and night.

GREENERY

A world of land and water, light and dark;
Swish! and hush! the waves against the rocks;
Swirling foam and twinkling glints; sh-shocks
Slap-slapping across the rippling arc, arc,

In widening rings of water; shimmering dance
Of light and shadow on the glittering waves;
Tower; flood back; power pours through the caves;
Regular rushes cling close in a rhythmic advance.

This world of motion and tricksy light and shade:
How long before the extra step was stepped?
How long the lullaby, until life leapt
And drifting molecules synthesis made?

Synthesis, photosynthesis; gradually greenery
- Unrecorded enrichment – added growth to the scenery.

SEA POWER

Twinkling ripples and patterns of foam through the rockpools,
Rush and lull as the wavelets advance and retreat,
With stately calm the ocean restores its dominion,
The steady surge, and the coolness caressing spent heat.

Deeper and deeper sways the triumphant water,
Confident swell and fall like a beating heart.
Weed, laid listless, lifts its arms to the movement.
At one with this kingdom, each living thing plays its part.

Life that was clamped and clenched in hidden protection,
The hard world of rocks and pebbles, grit and sand,
Now opens and feeds and flaunts itself under the water,
Drifting landscapes, feathery gardens, open-fanned.

Dry and dreary and desiccated, hearts that were lifeless,
When love returns, thrive and thrill and unfold.
Drab greys and browns and drying greens
Grow real again, silver and pink and emerald and gold.

But what of storm and power and towering anger
That rips the weed from the rocks, scatters boulders in rage?
Is that the work of love, or must we ignore it:
No place for destruction, on so sentimental a page?

Yeah, even the havoc has purpose, that shatters our equilibrium;
Gouges out silted-up channels; throws obstacles free;
Growling and grinding to break down the hard and the obstinate;
Gritty, sharp shingle? Sand, soft as silk, time shall see.

Boulders lie shattered and scattered, reveal secret treasure,
Undreamt-of riches of marble or gold.
Smashed fragments release hidden histories, fossil mysteries,
New understanding, to handle and hold.

A landscape transformed, new growth and new vigour;
New depths fill with beauty, frilling fronds, scuttling life.
Swirls through the rockpools the dance of the water,
Kiss of the working waves, peace after strife.

REPRISE : THE ENGLISH LAKE DISTRICT

- Homage to Impressionism –

World of mystery, where land and water
Tiptoe along the brink, to mingle in magic.
Mist smokes through the trees. The scene grows shorter
Closed off by curtains of rain, suddenly tragic;

Then lifting. Peep-oh to the sunshine! flashing
In rippling swathes across the lake. Grey
Drapes the hills in moving clouds, splashing
The scattered sunlight again. Oh, mixed-up magical day!

And the peace, the peace, of land and water,
Watching the light and shade among the hills:
Moments of gold, breezes from another quarter;
Gaps grey, then sunlit; showers the moment spills;

Trees, kissing the sky, welcome the gentle rain;
Trickles to the lake; then sparkling sunshine again.

OUT OF THE DARKNESS

What is as black as coal? Such total darkness,
Yet shining with rainbow sheen, as if in mockery;
Hard, yet brittle; jagged, crumbling squareness;
Useless for stone or bricks; faint-hearted trickery.

The beautiful forests of giant waving ferns,
Feet in the sultry swamp, fronds in the sky;
Heat from the brave young sun, and showers, by turns;
Energy factory, towering high.

The sun grew shrouded, that summoned them high:
Felled and fallen, those waving, whispering fronds;
Feeble and shrivelled under the darkening sky,
Choked and stifled in the silted ponds.

Pressured in fold on fold of black despair;
Helpless captives, squeezed of freedom and grace,
Those glorious giants that swept the air!
Bowed and broken, in confined space.

Suffocating! Helpless! Trapped in the dark!
What is essential? What must be retained?
Power being compacted: fuel for the spark.
Let all the rest go, as the ooze is drained.

Guarding the essence, while continents sank or rose;
Compressed into layers, while strata wrinkled and split;
The heave of earth's processes: birthing that shows
In value transformed, fossil energy stored, to be lit:

That black heart fired a revolution;
Powered the world for progress, speed and labour,
Travel, inventions: ideas to find the solution
To plague and famine; dyes, medicines; help our neighbour.

Now the black-hearted beauty fades into history.
Our thoughts are filled with fronds that waved in the sun.
Well-studied fossils reveal their palaeo-mystery:
The living world of giants whose work is done.

THE BLUEPRINT

The sleeping future, safe from harm,
Packed tight in grain or nut or tiny seed
Till times propitious; faithful, like a charm
The sprout shall shoot, obedient to its breed.

The past, with all its failures and success,
Selection and adaptation, wisdom of centuries,
Encapsuled; every detail, dot or recess
Encoded and enclosed, concealed from injuries.

Minute instructions, hidden, too small for sight,
Developed; in leaf and stalk and blossom and fruit,
Revealed and recognised; reality packed so tight,
The self that can't be denied, flows in the shoot.

Combining light and moisture, following its code,
Leaves spread in strength, then flowers, the crowning beauty,
Sweetness and scent and colour. As they fade, -
Discarded glamour, - the final workaday duty:

In its own grain, or nut, or tiny seed,
Transmit, for safety, the blueprint of its breed.

FRUIT

What use the blueprint, if materials lack?
Growth will need energy, easy for the eager germ.
The provident parent prepares a survival pack
For rapid release, when waiting has reached its term.

Faithful, as the flowers fade and the seed grows stronger,
The patient parent lifts its leaves to the light,
Harvesting strength, for its own growth no longer,
To endow a living legacy, future bright.

Fruit trees, symbol of nature's abundance,
Rustle the light, dappling the infant fruit,
Processing sugar, reaping the sundance,
To store round the seedcore, ready when seeds shall shoot.

Rainbow of fruit and berries, gushing with juice,
Delight to the eye, ecstasy on the tongue:
Tints and textures, packaged for practical use:
Moisture and energy, perfect for struggling young.

Grain, stuffed with starch, stores fuel for a hundred-fold,
To rise like a rocket, released by the warmth and wet.
Nuts guard their wealth behind walls, like a banker's stronghold.
Through frost and snow, they'll suffer many seasons yet.

Defences cracked, the naked naïve youngster
Rushes for the light, unfurling a bold seedleaf,
Oil from the kernel, fuel for this greedy guzzler,
Finding his feet, fast-launched in his leap for life.

Suddenly, for strawberries, slowly, for oaks,
Breeding will show in new generations,
When light invites and moisture soaks,
Greedily grateful for survival rations.

THE CHURCHYARD FLOODED WITH SNOWDROPS

The sombre thickets of summer
Where gloom forbids anything grow,
Transparently welcome late winter
With winter's white wealth: living snow.

White, because only white will do
To harvest the day's short light;
Pools of snowdrops, like extra snow,
Bless the chill soil, pure white!

Plain white, simple white, gentle white;
No perfume, just tipped with green;
True white, repeated white, unvarying;
Fallen sky lights the woodland scene.

Tangled twigs in the winter sky
Weave black and white high above;
On the ground this monochrome carpet,
Flora's first cautious move.

WINTER WALLFLOWER

Bonfire colours in the cold,
Tawny brown and yellow gold,
You should be sheltering from the storm
And wait until the spring turns warm.

You took a chance; You lost the bet;
Winter has hardly started yet.
The chill to blow your fire out
Is on its way. This wind has clout.

You dance and dip in falling snow,
Mere flying flakes that hardly show.
A heavier fall will make you droop
And lay you low, with all your troop.

I'll take a photo of your scene
Fluttering now, above the green;
And, e'er the frost can slay your pride,
I'll save you, in a vase, inside.

CYCLAMENS SETTLE IN

"They'll make themselves at home," said my cousin,
As we dug up cyclamens and wrapped them snug.
"You'll be weeding them out by the dozen,
Out of control, like a ragged Turkish rug."

"Not in York," was my thought, as we bagged them
On her sunny sloping hillside near the Lakes.
"They'll be lucky to survive, when I've dragged
them
East, to gloomy corners." Sunflash bakes

In sudden strikes, dry, across my garden.
Foliage wilts and yellows in a day.
Reflections from the windows cross, to harden
The soil and sizzle plants all in their way.

But cyclamens are tougher than I'd noticed.
They love the sun that scorches them back home.
They survive their Turkish winters, where, from
slopes, iced,
Then hot, through baking summers, tortoises roam.

Up through the lawn, unbothered by the wind,
First through the snow, they flourish without care.
In corners that I never thought they'd find:
Just look! Their cheeky pink is everywhere.

PULMONARIA

Not many flowers flaunt pink and blue
Together, on each stalk.
Here they flourish in double hue
Beside the shady walk.

Untidy, spreading, out of control,
They raise their pretty faces,
To welcome spring with heart and soul
In some of the gloomiest places.

Mary-and-Joseph, the country name
For this twin-coloured flower of March,
When the 19th honours the quiet saint
Who taught the Son of God so much,

And the 25th March is Lady Day,
When the angel brought Mary the news
Of Jesus' birth, and we hear her say:
"Let God do as He choose."

In summer, silver dots the leaves:
Pulmonaria, lungwort, the name;
But the old-fashioned name each spring receives
This boost, to remember the same.

So welcome the spreading blue and red,
Double colour for the holy pair.
Don't weed them all from your flowerbed.
Light the gloom: spring is everywhere.

LARKSPUR & NIGELLA

Larkspur and nigella are sprouting through the grass,
Frills of lacy leaves among the blades;
Sure the winter's over, sure the cold will pass,
Frolicking in the sunlight, till it fades.

Larkspur and nigella have colonised my lawn,
With softer dainty green among the bristles,
Daring me to trim them, leafless, clipped and shorn.
Will they spread so cheerful, when wind whistles?

And frost and or sleet return for March's bitter bite?
The game of warm and chill in early spring?
Have larkspur and nigella got the toughness for a fight
To bring the buds to bloom and do their thing?

For if they can survive it, or March stays softly warm,
I think, I might not mow my lawn this year.
A blessing on their wildness, this enterprising swarm,
Surging through my grass, with pretty cheer.

Out of the Dreaming Dark 18

STRAY VIOLETS

These violets have no mossy stone
To hide them from the eye.
On bare cement their seed has grown,
Wide open to the sky.

Where dust has gathered in a crack,
Nature has claimed a space.
Here on the concrete, fighting back,
These little flowers bring grace.

Handful of life and colour,
From tiny, random seed,
Display the beauty of nature,
Joyful, carefree weed.

FIRST BLOSSOM

Will we remember the tiny wealth of spring?
Dainty flowers that sprinkled every branch;
Hopeful pink and delicate white, they swing
In every breeze that makes the bushes dance.

Have we noticed perfect tiny structure:
Five rounded petals – Yes, they'll tumble soon
And spread a bridal carpet in the gutter
To briefly lift and light the muddy gloom.

Each tiny flower, an engineer's delight:
Those pointed stamens, like a fairy crown,
With jewels at each point, all fastened tight,
Lift pollen to the wind and perfume round.

Can angels grasp the beauty we enjoy?
Can senseless spirits see or touch or smell
God's works of art? Us humans must employ
Minds, hearts and tongues, our physical praise to swell.

ALPINE FLOWERS

Like tiny miracles they deck the scree,
Clumps, huddling for warmth on the bitter height.
The adamant rockface shuns them but they cling tight
On crevice and shingle, insisting, permission to be!

Offspring of sun and rock and mountain wind;
Fluttering bravely, fragile, on slender stems;
Yellow and white and pink, like cushions of gems
Displayed to the sun, against the bare mountain pinned.

Here, where the sun strikes strongly, they flaunt their joy
In rays undimmed by the pure mountain air;
Revelling in all that energy; sweetness to spare
For hovering insects; pocket paradise to enjoy.

Each clump, an island of life on the sterile rock:
Cushions of warmth and sound, sweetness and colour.
The mist comes curling round. Its silver vapour
Chills, but cannot kill. Grey shadows block

The splendour. Hide your eyes! The petals close,
Shielding their tender heart till warmth returns.
Sheltered through snow or shadow, patience earns
New dancing freedom, bright, when new sunshine glows.

In their hostile world, savouring the strongest light;
Glutton for the glorious rays; life at the limit;
Lifted to the source of life: nothing to dim it;
On every splintered ledge – triumphant sight!

SPRING PROMISE

I wander up the garden
And lean against the fence:
Five minutes' relaxation
When work gets too intense.

The sun has got his hat off;
The breeze has stayed in bed;
The cat is sprawled beside me,
Relaxed beside my tread.

Forget-me-nots are charming.
Pause and love the weeds:
Spring, with its luscious promise;
Last year's careless seeds.

Creamy yellow-rattle,
Purple honesty,
Imperial as a Roman
In gorgeous finery.

Forget the fence needs painting;
Ignore the broken gate;
Enjoy the early promise
Before it gets too late.

TULIPS I

The tulips lift their chalices to the sun,
Like guardsmen in the heat, straight yellow and red,
Cupping the sunshine, treasuring the spring's late run
In shining bowls' hot glow above the flowerbed.

Girdled in gorgeous silk, the rays are trapped,
Reflected inwards, like a satellite dish,
Focusing on the centre. Petals overlapped
In harlequin-lozenge shadows, guard and swish

The fondling light around the flower's future;
Ripening the pollen, with its vital code,
Warming the three-horned pistil. The rays that nurture
Rest lovingly awhile. May's evenings slowed.

At last the petals fade, in crippled decadence,
Colours of gloom, in stricken glory,
Tumbling one by one, that shrivelled elegance,
In bankrupt splendour, a tragic story,

But tiny seeds hold all that wealth
Invested safe for another season. Underground
The round and fattening bulb still stores, by stealth,
This spring's rich hoard, increasing like a miser's mound.

TULIPS II*

The red runs round the rim of the white petals
As though you'd run out of ink, or, in a hurry
To blaze the garden, left this fringe till it settles:
You've skimped this clump! – Away! in a rainbow flurry.

The pearly white glows like a shape of shell,
Positive in its purity, here in its corner,
Hoarding the spring light in its upturned bell:
Luminous promise of sun growing warmer.

The black stamens wait, with their gypsy glance;
Languorous depth of every tulip's cup.
Brimming with chequered light, fêting the year's advance,
April's gorgeous guests hold their goblets up.

The jewelled blaze of mauve and gold and ruby,
Spring's trooping pageant, throngs each flowerbed;
But here, you were mean, and etched a finer beauty:
Pure polished white, outlined in careful red.

**Alas, the red-rimmed white tulip died before I took a photo, so here is a tulip's dying gloom.*

THE IRIS

Leaves like swords and stalks of steel,
Such structure and such strength!
Stoic, aloof, though the breezes reel,
Dancing the garden's length.

Imperial colours! Our crowns unfold
Their structure to the world:
Three arching hoops, chenille of gold,
Three silken tongues unfurled.

Purple or gold, white, mauve or browns,
Late spring's ten-day parades;
Maroons and blues, our velvet crowns,
Plumed regiments' shape and shades.

Sweeps of van Gogh glory;
Prima ballerina glints;
Stiff-drilled corps de ballet
In fluttering Degas tints.

Posing here, in satin skirts,
With arms raised like a dancer;
Hearing your praise, while the breeze flirts
Around me, here's my answer:

“I had no choice, by nature's law,
To spread my silk so fine.
Just to be me: all the year's store,
All my plant's show, is mine.

“I spread myself in beauty's place.
I hold myself serene.
Admirers come. Bees hum. My space
Is theirs as well. Our scene

“Will not last long. Sunshine and showers
Will bless some other parade.
Admirers grieve: ‘Such spectacular flowers!
What a shame, how quickly they fade!'

“Now the swords can rust; rhizome sun itself
All summer, to strengthen and harden;
But I have been my ten-day self
And graced my place in the garden.”

Out of the Dreaming Dark 23

OBEDIENT SERVANTS

Herb bennet and herb robert, two old friends,
Wait for the nature class, permitted weeds
Crowding the shingle, wild, where the garden ends.
"Look, class, the characteristics that nature breeds!

"What is the same, what different in these two plants?"
Both under knee-high, both springing from a floppy rosette;
Tough, slender, branching stems, highways for the ants;
Leaves: dark green, glossy, or fretted into dainty net.

Red-dipped, the lace-work; bristly, the glossy green;
Symmetrical, the lace-work; off-centre, the bristling point
Mounting from rounded base-leaves, same hairy sheen.
"Now, what's the arithmetic when we examine each joint?"

Herb bennet, two branches, leaf curled around the node.
Herb robert, five branches, two lifting leaves of lace.
Herb bennet, one branch continues in branching mode.
Herb robert, two branches still branching, criss-crossing the space.

Last, from each joint, the tiny, five-petalled flowers:
Singly on bennet, rounded, in cheery yellow;
Seedhead, a bristling burr, in ambush towers;
Twins for Robert, more delicate than his fellow:

In fairy pink, tooth-lipped and veined with red,
The tight-eyed flowers sprinkle the shaggy lace.
The pointed bill spears out when petals are shed.
Five coiling springs shall fling the seeds to their new place.

"Leaf and stem and flower and seed: Look class! Think!
All show their identity, you can't get them wrong;"
Still branching, tiny yellow and tiny pink;
Herb bennet and herb robert, all summer long.

COFFEE-BREAK ON THE ALLOTMENT

When you are tired of worthy cabbages,
And bored with crinkly feel and dark green flavour;
When you resent the times you trudge the ridges,
All burdened down with tedious, useful labour;

Deflate a while and take a smaller view;
Step down among the little things of life;
Under the useful crops, let's find a few
Self-planted weeds, not destined for the knife.

Heartsease! Tiny fatface! Gorgeous imp!
Purple and white and yellow, all in each flower!
And henbit, dragon, pink among the limp
Bibs of green; and pimpernel's scarlet power.

Germander speedwell drapes the soil with blue;
Straggly chickweed lifts its stars of white.
Groundsel stands straight, tufty bittercress too
And baby nettles sprout with shaggy spite.

A smaller view lets fun run the estate,
So let ten minutes' wildness fire your sorrow;
Let forceful smell and bulging roundness wait:
The cabbages will still be there tomorrow!

YELLOW AND BLUE

Oxford ragwort in shaggy gold
Lounges under my columbines. His ragged crowns
In tumbled heaps, took hold
In flowerbed and heart, when town's
New house and empty garden had spaces
Vacant for a cheery rascal
With gold to fling.
Now those grinning faces
Complement the columbines.
The end of spring
No blenching pastel:
Blazing blues and gold combine
- The ballerinas and the rascal –
A tapestry of hues divine,
Lasting for weeks, till fluffy seedheads
And crunchy pods must be culled quickly,
Not choke the ground, by falling thickly.

Guest ballerinas and welcome weeds
Have places now to show their graces.
No need to overwhelm us with seeds!

THE SCARLET POPPIES' DREAM OF PARADISE

God is the perfect poppy, purest scarlet,
Furnace of blazing colour, flame on a stalk,
And, central sensuality, the dark
Stamens, black mascara'd like a starlet.

Oh, the winking rhapsody, the fire;
Sultry attraction, ruddy cheerfulness;
The heat, the dance, the swaying loveliness,
The harvest sun, blue skies, fulfilled desire.

Redness complete, in shining sensuous silk;
Riding the breeze, full blown, in glorious being;
The droning bees, the rustling silk, agreeing
Every launched wish, bright Poppy o' the Ilk.

Scarlet poppies' nirvana! Do they ever think
Heretic pink poppies say: *God is pink!*

THREE ROSES

There are roses under the rowan tree,
Where no roses ought to be,
Although there are only three.

In the corner under the fence
Pearly white shines so intense
Among the shadows dense.

The parent bush is yards away.
Romping adventure led them astray.
This is the final spray.

Hundreds in bloom on the parent bush.
Pinker buds and pearly blush.
These three escaped the crush.

Secret, under the rowan tree;
Light in the shadows; only three,
Where no roses ought to be!

AUTUMN ROSES

The bush I pruned the hardest
Is flowering fit to burst.
No slowing down for autumn;
The gales can do their worst.

These peachy-yellow roses,
A shade my mum loved best,
Unstoppable all summer,
Don’t intend to rest.

I pruned them last November
And yet again in March
When spring winds ripped the foliage.
I worried I’d hacked too much.

But all the months of summer
They’ve flowered on ‘Repeat’,
Unheeding of the rainstorms,
Regardless of the heat.

The roses bounce like bridesmaids
In ballerina skirts.
Our hearts skip as we pass them.
Their fragrance flaunts and flirts.

So when life prunes you hardest
Don’t think it’s for the worst.
Gobble through the compost.
You’ll blossom, fit to burst.

DAY'S EYES

Daisies sprinkle the grass, like families,
Spreading their little welcome to the sun;
Yellow and white, no fuss, spread colonies,
Cheerful and bright, till sunshine's gone.

Each flower a commune of circled florets,
Fringes of white round yellow eyes,
Bristling ranks stand thick as a forest,
Tiny, five-pointed, pollen as their prize.

Each circle in turn entices boldly,
Like a ring of candles, target for the bees.
Each tiny pistil protrudes proudly,
Greedy for gold, by insects or breeze.

The scattered coronets close at the day's end,
Dutiful retreat into folded buds.
Lying on the leaves, like a spilt necklace,
Dewdrops glitter round the dark green studs.

The cheery faces on their stubby stalks
Forgive the mower, with its gnashing teeth.
Fresh ranks spring up to deck the walks,
Last week's mowings, scattered underneath.

Day in, day out, the day's-eyes follow the sun;
Resurgent fan-club, contracted for a nine-month run.

PLANTING SCHEMES

Silver and gold, the riverbank,
Planned by an artist mind;
Mirrored in the tranquil river
Where slow reflections wind:

Feathery green of tansy,
Feathery grey between,
Stroked by the summer breezes:
Picturesque pastoral scene!

Tansy's trays of florets,
Tufty yellow studs;
Silver plumes of mugwort,
Fringe above the floods.

When tansy turns to copper,
Warm in the autumn sun,
Mugwort still swaying silver,
Reflected in the river's run;

Disorderly profusion,
Nature's exuberant weeds,
Scattered in natural confusion:
Beauty the expert heeds:

Strolling along the riverbank,
The TV gardener's advice:
“Mix and contrast the foliage,”
Unrolls before our eyes.

DAFFODILS – PATIENCE

By July, the beds are empty;
The tattered leaves have gone;
The gold: a forgotten memory,
That danced in the early sun.

Spring's green growth has been processed.
The bulbs are full and round;
Now: half a year of silence,
Waiting, under the ground.

Eight months of nothing, in darkness;
Suspended animation!
Inert, unnoticed, meaningless,
Entombed for summer's duration.

Pansies, delphiniums, roses,
Fill the hot days with colour;
Dahlias, as the year closes,
Lengthen the reign of summer.

Nothing stirs for the daffodil,
True to its trust, in the dark;
Gardens are swept by winter chill;
In the black soil, not a mark!

But tiny leaves stand ready,
Formed in the bulb's faithful heart.
As new spring totters, unsteady,
The rising spears make a start.

While spring still throws us a mixture
Of sleet and breeze and sun,
The daffodils dance us a picture:
Golden life, risen again!

WILD MULLEIN

Between the railway tracks the mullein stands,
A four-foot challenge to the gardener's skill.
Spire of grey and yellow! What demands,
To lure you in, must flowerbeds fulfil?

Bees throng busily round the tempting spike,
Finding the scattered yellow among the grey,
Ignoring the shuffling goods train's lazy swipe:
Tall candles for a drowsy summer's day.

Colourscheme from nightmares! Purple or red
Ferocious stamens snarl in the yellow face;
Noxious fascination! Won't you, instead
Of waste and shingle, flower in some cherished space?

This bristling purple and the gentle yellow
Deserve the richest compost, gardener's pride:
A feature in the border; silver fellow
In dusky gloom, at soft astilbe's side.

But surfeit of good compost makes you struggle,
Swamped by good things, too rich a diet here!
A Spartan life for you! Out on the shingle
Between the railway tracks you raise your spear.

Yet, still, among the lazy crazy paving,
Or where some trendy planner has spread the pebbles
For textured weed-control – such a saving
Of time and labour! – to stifle the gardener's troubles,

On this new-fangled waste you lift your spear.
For nature, banished, you reclaim her sphere!

LAST POPPY

These poppies found a crack
To raise their blue-grey sculpture,
The garage at its back.
Here is a shout for Nature.

A seed as small as dust
Ferried the gift of life,
Blown on a wayward gust
By the Gardener in chief.

Two months I have ignored it,
Although I weeded grass,
While leaves grew, and root bored its
Way, where my feet pass.

Huge poppies, fluttering mauve,
Have opened wide, and fallen;
Low down, bruise-eyed – dear love, –
Bashful and faint, the last one.

My flowerbeds have yielded
None of the seeds I threw.
Just here, pale and unheeded,
Random and strong, here's you!

THE FIRST CHINESE LANTERN

In the back corner of August,
Glinting behind green leaves,
Orange elf-glow signals autumn:
Last call! for the slumping sheaves.

Old friend! So nice to see you!
I've missed you! Where have you been?
But pain drags at my welcome:
Year's end is moving in.

Full summer lingers, drowsy,
Sprawling in the heavy sun,
But your flame is lit in the shadows
To signal his time is done.

Your strings of orange lanterns
Will brighten the dying year,
Autumn's glowing embers
As the final shades draw near.

Green still reigns in the gardens;
Nights have not yet turned hazy;
But, tip-toe, you've lit your lantern,
While summer still holds us, lazy.

CHINESE LANTERNS

God the engineer has kept us waiting
But late in summer, slowly, to his plan
The rods of lanterns fill, like fairy ladders.
Green pales to orange, darkens, crispens. Man

Must plan and build and cut and trim and rivet;
Measure his angles, fret and fume and leave
And come again, pick up again, restart it;
Fix every strut; then test and shove and heave;

But perfectly, and shapely, every lantern,
With every vein and fibre in its place,
Has grown, from fallen flower, to sturdy structure,
Light-weight and strong. Inside its shining space,

Rounded, in cosy light, the fruit is warm,
Ripening slowly, safe, till the lampshades wither
And, final brilliance! in the netted cage
The orange berry gleams: same shining colour!

NASTURTIUMS

Why did I weed you out? Your autumn fire
Is what the borders need. Scarlet and gold
Run rampant, through the fence, along the wire,
You fill the gaps. Stop summer growing old.

And here the bees I haven't seen all year
Are bumbling, fumbling, busy at your lips
And zipping down your throats. To your long rear
You tempt them, tubes with nectar at the tips.

Four generations since I planted you
And heaved you out among the plants you flattened.
Now, weakened, corralled, I'll give you your due:
We need this bonfire, on the wall you've brightened.

Obstinate friend, just scatter a few seeds
To jazz us up next year, as autumn needs.

Out of the Dreaming Dark 31

COSMOS

Like big expanded daisies, or sunflowers, quarter-size,
Cosmos fill the borders and spread their petals wide.
Compositae, a community, aloft upon each stem,
Disc florets in the centre, rim florets round the rim.

Rim florets work the hardest, extending one coloured finger,
Crimson, pink or glowing white, to summon guests to linger,
The final treats of summer, sweetness, fertility, strength,
Late joy for hovering insects, roving the garden's length.

Ring by ring the inner florets open, each in turn,
Each golden prong of pollen dust, gripped in a tiny urn,
Circles of golden prickpoints, nectar in each cup,
Progressing towards the centre, while outsides shrivel up.

Hoverflies buzz dreamily; nectar and pollen tempt;
Golden days of autumn stretch summer's lazy length.
Every tiny floret has a task it cannot shirk:
To set a seed, 'gainst winter chill, so spring can set to work.

 Out of the Dreaming Dark 32

PASSIONFLOWER

I might have dug the garden.
I might have planted peas
Or sprouts or beans or carrots,
To pick and eat or freeze,

But I just planted flowers
And mowed the lawn between:
Colour in every season
And never-ending green.

Before I'd even started,
Or scraped the shingle out,
Against the neighbour's hedges,
Sprang up a cheeky sprout.

“Aha,” I thought, “I know you.”
Despite two winters' snow,
I watched that passionflower
Clamber up and grow.

The flower itself's a marvel,
With whiskers white and blue.
Bees come. That means honey!
Hoverflies visit too.

Finally, among the foliage,
In late September heat,
The hanging fruit shine orange:
I have grown something to eat!

SLOES*

Are you trying to hide?
Why choose such dusty blue?
Hidden among the prickles
This hue gives not a clue.

You’re clinging to your thorns
As though you are afraid
To be hung out to ripen.
You’d rather keep the shade.

This tint gives not a hint
That here is fruit worth eating.
You’re draped in shady shadows,
Dark like a bruise from beating.

Winter’s on its way,
With rain and snow to wash you;
With frost to break your skin
And split and spill and squash you.

As jams or gin or wine,
I know we’d all approve you.
Just let me get you home
Where everyone will love you.

**Sloes are a species of wild plums, very sour till frost changes them.*

OAK LEAVES

Every leaf has done its work
And now it says farewell;
Tumbled in the gutter,
Still with a name to tell.

Jagged, like dragons' fingers;
Crisper than the rest;
Dry, but the message lingers:
"Ancient oak, we're the best."

Almost a deliberate pattern:
Pale oakleaves, dull dusty beech;
Just as the breeze has scattered
And piled the last of each.

Did I notice the oak tree
All summer, against the sky?
Now, its leaves bear witness.
Here at my feet they lie.

Is it millions, or merely thousands
Of leaves, cast on the wind,
To bequeath their worth, as compost
And leave a name behind?

AUTUMN LEAVES

You keep your faith. It's in your DNA,
Spread out in every leaf across my path;
True as King Arthur's knights to loyal oath
Your oak and ash and chestnut on display.

We can ID you all, where here you lie,
Telling the truth with every kink and wrinkle,
Tracing the curves of oak, or crispy crinkle
Too-early-fallen chestnut, crunched and dry.

You tell us of your troubles: summer drought,
Leaves falling early; or the sucking pests
Draining the chestnut. Feeble giant rests
Before his time and can't see summer out.

In shape of leaf, last signature of trust,
Consign your outline to the waiting dust.

ALOE FLOWER

Subtle palette of untrue colours;
Soft orange, too timid to blaze;
Tints for the fringe of the desert,
That blench and blend in the haze.

Awkward blue-grey of leaves and stem,
Like bottle-green, betrayed;
Purse-lipped flowers, tipped with green,
Clutch nectar. There's no shade.

You belong where the sun-dried colours
Falter in the bleaching light;
Citizens of sand and pebbles
Where the desert threatens: dry! blight!

Clinging, in the hot savannah,
Like sculptures, those strange leaves curled;
Tough; leathery; wrung waterskins;
Hostile in a hostile world.

Hues of the wild open spaces,
Where hyenas howl in the hills
And the sand is harsh in the sunlight,
Flower on our windowsills.

NEGATIVE PERFECT

Does nature smile in the mirror
And hug herself at the joke,
That shows us the beauty of negative
In darkness, like sooty soft smoke?

Lilies and swans for purity,
Gleaming spotless white,
But if you turn the world over:
Be amazed at the beauties of night!

Negative swans, in beauty,
Glide with a coal-black gleam.
Beside them a gloomy swamp lily
Reflects like a ghoul in the stream.

We love the white, in its glory,
A positive picture of peace,
But the black has just the same quality,
Serene and shining. They please

As much in their dazzling darkness
From the world turned upside-down,
As ours, in their dazzling whiteness:
Stuff of legend and renown.

Would Leda have loved her seducer
If he'd wooed her in villainous black?
Would Adonis lie among lilies
Dull as bruises, for Venus' attack?

They would, if they'd seen this loveliness,
Gloom in a glorious mode:
The shining spathe of the lily;
Sooty swansdown, soft for her brood.

The dark side has truth to teach us,
Subverting established ideas:
Re-consider the truth of opposites;
Look again at our nightmare fears.

Congratulations, Australia!
But! A final problem I speak:
The white arum lily breathes sweetness;
Swamp lilies waft a rancid reek.

Note: Long after writing this poem I learnt that the swamp or dragon lily comes from SE Asia-- or even the lands around the Mediterranean Sea

Out of the Dreaming Dark 36

BANANAS

They're all just yellow! Bananas!
(Though some are green, or speckly brown)
And that half-hearted bend, tease or charm us,
-- Comes from growing upside-down!

Did you know they're sterile? Bananas?
Just a pointless store of starch.
Fruitless fruit, without seed. Why harness
Hot sun, swishing rain? Greedy arch!

As it bends to the earth, growing riper,
The swag nearly touches the ground.
A burglar would stagger, to swipe a
Hoard, stacked so high, that he'd found.

Such betrayal of pollinators' roaming,
When the bats came flitting through the dusk;
Pale petals glimmering in the gloaming;
Wasted journey! No seedling! Bloated husk!

But when a hopeful sucker
Comes proddling from a distant root
Greedy for some farmyard muck or
Anything, to feed the new shoot,

That's when some hoarded riches
Might drop, overripe, from the sky,
And, powered by the rotting sweetness,
The young shoot grows towering high.

A bit of lateral thinking!
Mother nature's sleight of hand:
The stooping fertilizer, sinking
Over new growth, struggling from the sand.

So, if your work seems pointless,
Sterile, dispirited, lost,
Watch out for sky-high compost
Dumped where you need it most.

They're not just a joke! Bananas!
Another way of coping: a surprise!
So let the yellow bendy fruit charm us,
Full of energy! Stored from the skies!

* Find out about other bananas, and why only the sterile yellow ones are familiar in importing countries.

GOURDS & PUMPKINS

All these pretty pumpkins, for pies or soup or tarts;
Stuffed, or chopped for chutney, or sweetened for desserts;
The best will lie here, lazy, prized for looking good,
Kept as decoration by artists, who love a gourd;
While those who know the secret, to dry them really well,
Will shake the seeds, to rattle, as good as a country bell.
There's still time, Cinderella. The best are growing still.
No need to pine for a pumpkin! No desperate tears to spill!
Just leave the rats and mice on guard, while you sweep up the ashes;
They'll get you to the ball on time, no matter what the rush is.
Heroines' transport of choice; fairy godmothers appear;
Glamorous role for a pumpkin; sparkling end to the year.

FUNGI!

There is a time for fungi! Among the fallen leaves,
When autumn gloom laments the harvest's end;
The orchards have been emptied; gathered, the golden sheaves;
The dripping darkness has no more to spend,

No wealth to offer, just the vanishing gold
Of autumn squelch. All's finished. All is wrecked.
Birds sing a hopeless note. Among the old
Dark conifers, what life can we expect . . . ?

Nature again in triumph! Children's joy!
An enigmatic flourish, who knows where?
Sprouting up unexpected: kill or enjoy:
Sweet pixy houses, or the toad's death chair.

Riches another gathered: tree or shrub:
Leaves, dead, that processed light from the distant sun;
Patient complexity, to synthesise from rub-
Bish; quintessent chemistry. The year is run!

Underground re-processing: optimize nature's kindness:
Death, or strong medicine, out of the gloom,
Re-cycling scraps of fallen goodness.
There is a time for fungi! Leave them room.

late-winter fungi

~~~ DAY 4 ~~~

And God said,
"Let's have lamps in the arch of the sky, to
separate the day from the night,
and let them serve as signs
to mark festivals, and days and years.
Let them be lamps in the dome of the sky to
give light on the earth."

And that's what happened.
God made two huge lamps—
the larger lamp to rule the day
and the smaller lamp to rule the night.
He made the stars too.

God arranged them all in the dome of the sky
to give light on the earth,
to organise the day and the night,
and keep light separate from darkness.
And God gave it His approval.
Evening was followed by morning—
the fourth day was complete.

Book of Genesis 1,14-19

INTO FOCUS: THE SUN

Living by the pattern of day and night,
Gradually we make the pieces fit,
Recognising: What **is** the source of light?
We get things into focus bit by bit.

The sun seemed like an extra, only for bright days,
Pegged in the sky like a Christmas bauble;
Left in the cupboard during rain or haze.
No part to play if the weather is troubled;

Learning, it's always there, even when hidden
Behind the clouds: the sun is the source of day!
All our light and energy, returning unbidden.
Morning till evening, shining on work and play;

Light can reach us, even through cloud and rain.
Love can touch us, even through grief and pain.

LUNAR EXPLORATION

Inconstancy the question first provokes:
The fickle moon: why sometimes? Where does it go?
Full beam, silvering the night with gleaming spokes,
Or slim, or vanished, blackness and dim starglow.

Painted by poets in sweeps of silver and black,
Serene and delicate world of the mirroring moon;
Magic so brief, before the dark floods back,
Light so ethereal, romantic, vanishing soon.

Wondering humans count the full moonlit nights;
The fading, the dark nights, new sliver, fattening again;
Recognise a trusty pattern in the varying lights:
Gradual, reliable, retiring, returning again.

No moon: no moonlight! Science takes first steps
Looking for answers, coupling cause and effect;
Calculate, anticipate; the long journey to partnership;
Harnessing creation; superstition becomes respect.

Poets and scientists both owe duty –
Silver coin tribute – to the moon's changing beauty.

WIFELY ADVICE

the Moon speaks

(overheard a few days before 11 Aug 1999)

"Yes, dear, I know,
You shine on them all the time,
Day in,
Day out,
And never a word of gratitude;
Year in,
Year out,
Utterly reliable,
And nobody takes a bit of notice.

Now, if you threw a monthly,
Like I do,
There'd be all sorts of fuss;
Or if your light were gentler,
-- Oh no, I'm not criticising!
Oh, I know, it's natural to be strong!
Yes, I know,
That's what they take for granted,
Whereas I'm so weak, they think it's poetic.
-- All sorts of drivel they write!

So if you just let me get in front of you,
Just for two minutes,
Not very often,
Then they'll make a fuss,
-- No, it's not me they'll be fussing about.

They might even put you on the telly!"

-- Solar eclipse, over Cornwall 11.11.am

DAY AND NIGHT

The patient in and out of day and night:
A time for work and play, a time for sleep,
A time for spaces, freedom, colours bright,
A time for cosy closeness, quiet, deep.

“Where does the day go?” The wondering child
Knows they have passed, like pages of a book
Turned over and finished, stored perhaps in a pile
To be used again, when we know where to look.

“Why does the night come?” Already the little one knows
That light won't last forever; day returns;
But night brings an end to action. Silence grows:
A world calmed down, switched off. Inaction burns.

But: action and inaction, step by step,
We build our lives, and slowly climb their peak.
Question by following question, we unwrap
This gift, our world; stretching by the answers we seek.

LAMPS IN THE SKY

REGULATION!

It's regulations day:
Light can't flick on and off without a reason.
Let's get the wiring right
To mark each day and year and month and season.

Day Two, we underpinned, and fixed the sky;
Day Three, the garden;
Now it's time to get the designers in.
Let's get a move on!

Lamps, and colourschemes; patterns of stars
To make sense of the sky!
"I want a homely effect, without losing the feeling of space."
"That's quite a good try."

And did one opt for green, and tranquillity?
But some of the team insisted on red and gold?
And were allowed to do autumn: *"so long as it's quick!"*
Then a complete strip-down:
-- *"Nakedness is so truthful!"* –
Till the restart after the cold.

Then, the paperwork,
When all has settled down and found its place.
"Now counting can really begin!"
"And soon we'll have a wondering, measuring, calculating, organising, ***re****-decorating, human race."*

WINTER

Show us the bare essentials, the strong shapes
Of the land, stripped of its covering; no distraction
From colour, to ease and please; just wispy mist drapes
And arrays the landscape in layers, laid out for inspection.

Ridges and clefts unknown in the summertime,
Strength or scars that the leaves concealed,
Roll and dip in austere monochrome,
Raw in their majesty, patterns of hedge and field.

The trees stand naked in rattling latticework,
Stately structures of power and grace,
Each species unique; the fan-like openwork
Combing the sky, fingering, filling their space.

New understanding, viewing the land in its emptiness;
New recognition, each skeleton tree displayed;
No claim on our love, from colour or comfort or sweetness,
Just a naked old friend, showing how strength was made.

SPRING

The dancing spring, tossed in the sparkling wind;
Strands of fragrance weaving through the air,
Gusting around, assailing us from behind,
Leading us through the sunshine, showing us where

Shaken tassels are showering gold.
Sunshine and gold dust scatter the gleaming twigs,
Wychhazel and catkins, defying the cold,
In swirling sunshine, decking the sprigs.

Birds furnish the bareness with their songs,
Extra value each tumbling, chirruping note,
Filling the waiting spaces. Rights and wrongs,
Little-bird joys and sorrows pour from each throat.

Timid shoots peep shyly from the earth –
Leatherlike timid! Tough against snow or frost;
Snatching each moment of warmth; brilliant birth
Of tiny glories, glowing when needed most.

Snowdrops, crocuses, celandines starting the year
With blazing success, undeterred by the biting wind.
Trees toss the sunshine. Skies cloud and clear
Through filtering twigs, still silver behind.

With perfume and breeze and silver and gold and emptiness
Birdsong launches the year into beauty and busyness.

LATE SPRING

May, like a blousy teenager,
Knee-deep in froth of Queen Anne's lace,
Festoons the country lanes in tossing blossom.
In city too, like frowning dowager,
With dubious taste,
She preens in mauve and yellow, all showy and handsome.

The trees, like vertical flowerbeds,
Unroll their banners above the roads;
Parade in every shade of white and pink.
Joyfully, every breeze sheds
Petals and perfume, fairyland clouds,
Swirling confetti for brides on the brink.

Millions of flowers
Sway on the branches and drift from on high,
Blending the ground and sky in coloured distraction.
Tinted showers
On shoulder and pavement scatter and fly.
One flower on my sleeve draws my attention.

Here, in sheer perfection,
Such tiny detail winks a lashy eye:
Roundy-petalled may, with red-tipped whiskers.
Wilder, a Chinese dragon
From chestnut candles in the sky
Tumbles his fiery way to join his sisters.

Laburnum's yellow cascades:
Every pea-lipped flower perfect;
Lilac's tufted cockades:
Tiny crosses, cupped, protect.

Grinning lace-faces
Foam in the hedgerows in billowing abundance:
Veils for the graces,
Flung and flaunted with innocent extravagance.

Among the curtseying swags,
May bows and flirts,
Ruffling the frills and flounces
Of her dancing skirts.

SUMMER, 1950s

Cosy gloom of the attic where we play:
Outside, the heavy grey clouds are threatening rain,
Rain, rain again, cloaking the summer's day,
Like a friendly uncle, ruler of this chill domain.

Sweet summer's empire rarely touches this coast.
Caressing fingers retreat from the north-east wind;
Snatched from his nibbling breath and muddling mist
To safer haunts: snug, cosseted valleys, inland;

So, under that sheltering cloak, what lives we led!
Cowboys and Indians galloped from the dressing-up box.
Princesses screamed. Dragons growled to be fed.
Dancers twirled. Designers adjusted old frocks.

Personalities bloomed amid the lace and feathers,
Happy activity, squabbles, compromise, kindness;
Safe and dry, ignoring the outside weather's
Rage, or sulks, drumming raindrops, grey blindness.

Now endless sunshine beams on us from the telly:
The packaged, fantasy world of Australian soap.
Such unreality! Turning our lives to jelly.
No interaction! No involvement, to teach us to cope.

Those chill, grey summers sheltered a world of fun,
Living and growing, oblivious of rain or sun.

MEDITERRANEAN SUMMER

Hibiscus! Colour of life in a still world!
World of petrified heat between white walls;
Dry cage of stillness; Silence, as foot falls
On muting gravel; Leaves hanging, not a breeze curled.

Too hot for beetles, birds, any living thing;
A world of stone and heat and deathly calm;
Life has closed up; no sound, no breath of balm;
All essence desiccated. Here you fling

Your trumpet-note of brightness, scarlet, white-veined,
Living and strong and delicate, like a maiden's hand;
Life's plenipotentiary, full-powered, command
All stakes in the vacant air. Life can't be drained!

Red! Alive! A trumpet in the silent heat,
Focussing joy and hope in the empty street.

AUTUMN

I loved your works already, marvelled
At leaves fringed with hoar like glittering fretwork,
Heart-aching pinks and browns, as the garden shrivelled
Into grateful rest, spiders' webs a diamond network.

Even decay has glory, shrouded in peace,
Still pleasing, with its varied contours and berries of flame.
Round or straight, shiny or shaggy, at ease,
The leaves lie comfortably, returning whence they came.

Who taught me the beauty of fading greens and browns?
Elsewhere, the wild glory of flying red and gold:
Autumn, riotous or peaceful. The sodden path drowns
My footsteps. In the quiet, solitude takes hold.

Your company; our gaze together; in peace I gather
The memories, the promises, of autumn, with you, Father.

Out of the Dreaming Dark 48

NOVEMBER POEM

When all the saints go marching in,
And all's left brown and bare,
And all the soggy remnants
Just speak of our despair:

All the gold and orange
Lies squelching underfoot;
Harvest's been stripped into storage,
Greens and grain and fruit;

Above the blotched horizon
The bird flocks sweep and swoop,
Speckling the lonely skyline:
Landscape without hope.

But have you seen the chestnuts?
And have you seen the oaks?
And have you seen the alders
By the stream your sorrow chokes?

For every leaf that's fallen,
The scar is grey and healed;
A new bud, fat and swollen:
New year's fresh hope, still sealed;

So where the saints went marching,
The trees won't long be bare.
We all gestate God's kingdom
And we will do our share.

~~~ DAY 5 ~~~

And God said,

"Let the water teem with living creatures,
and let birds fly above the earth
and through the sky."
That's how God created
every kind of sea creature, large and small,
according to their species,

and every winged bird and flying creature,
species by species.

And God gave them His approval.

God blessed them and said,

"Be fruitful and multiply
and fill the water in the seas,
and let the birds and flying things
multiply on the earth."

Evening was followed by morning—

the fifth day was complete.

Book of Genesis 1, 20-23

LIMITS

Alien element where breath is threatened,
Beautiful and dangerous, powerful or still,
In your rocking, first lives were begotten.
Sealed beneath your surface, they have their own world still.

Masters of their universe, the silent fish
Glide gracefully, keeping pace with each other;
A flick, and all turn; a shadowy swish
Down-current, or 'cross it; Manoeuvres? No bother!

Thousands or millions in close formation
Follow the pattern of seasons and tides,
At home, in *their* element. Mystification,
Deceptive reflections, each other world hides.

Not one life-system sprang from God's word,
But two, inter-acting, yet different, occurred.

CORAL REEF

Like flowers let loose, bright fish with patterns
Roam and wander through the coral reef;
Red, yellow, black, through living rock curtains,
Stone florists' displays; a place for each brief
Or centuries-old lifeform, tethered or free;
Slow-motion universe, in warm, shallow sea.

THE TIDAL ZONE

Two regimes in conflict
Alternate twice a day,
Offering the opposites:
Close contact or airy indifference.
Drenching, swirling water
With nuzzling, kissing sway:
This might pull and drag you,
Legless, into depths where you have no chance!

Air has no force to pull you.
You cower, undisturbed,
Clamped close against the dryness,
Anchored tight, or buried in sand;
But this peace has nothing to offer;
Here comes the hungry bird.
Oh, for the circling water,
Nourishment and freedom, grand!

Growing up in a war zone,
The soft lives of the shore
Harden to the warring forces,
Grab what existence they can;
Inside their rocklike protection,
Survival, and nothing more;
First law: to protect their weakness;
Invulnerable; alone.

Not here the social network
Of family life, or clan:
Mutual interdependence
For rearing, play or hunt.
Armoured individuals,
Immovable, so nothing can
Penetrate a tender corner,
Touch them, for love or hurt.

The clash of enemy forces,
Drying air, or swish of sea –
So many human children
Are caught by the raging tides!
Hardened by others' conflict
Who can help them to be
Warm and loving and tender,
All that the armour hides?

SEA MONSTERS

The great sea-monsters of nightmare and legend
Vanish, in a puff of reality.
No sea-dragons writhing, just friendly, threatened
Whales, whose hunting was history;

But the tiny terrors at the water's edge
Are monsters we take for granted.
Have you studied them in the fringe
Of seaweed, dark forests! Enchanted!

Soft lives in armour, monopods, bivalves:
A world of feeding feet:
The foot-mouths graze under the waves,
Ravenous after drought and heat.

Anemones wave their tentacles.
Nothing can escape their clutches.
Other horrors extrude their stomachs
To surround their prey, ingest their lunches.

Out of the Dreaming Dark 51

Starfish, cucumbers, zany frilled worms,
Hermit crabs in borrowed homes;
Things we can't see, betrayed by the squirms
Of sand where the clear ripple foams;

Sea-urchins, sucking octopi,
-- Mini-sized, round Britain's coast –
Drilling oyster-catchers, menace from the sky;
Lurking lobsters; Horror, the most!

The crab waves his eyes and sidles past
Like a drunk, with evil intent.
The vicious nippers will grab on fast,
Then scurry away; find a dent

Under the rocks, to ambush and plunder
Guzzling food as it passes.
Cool camouflage: dark green shell, hiding under
Dark green seaweed; fool the nature classes!

Don't forget the terrors of this world of monsters,
As you drop your hoard in a bucket.
Be grateful for the nightmare reduced to funsters,
Cut down to size, so you can take it.

Keep a sense of humour, to help you see,
Even in the nightmare, God's mastery.

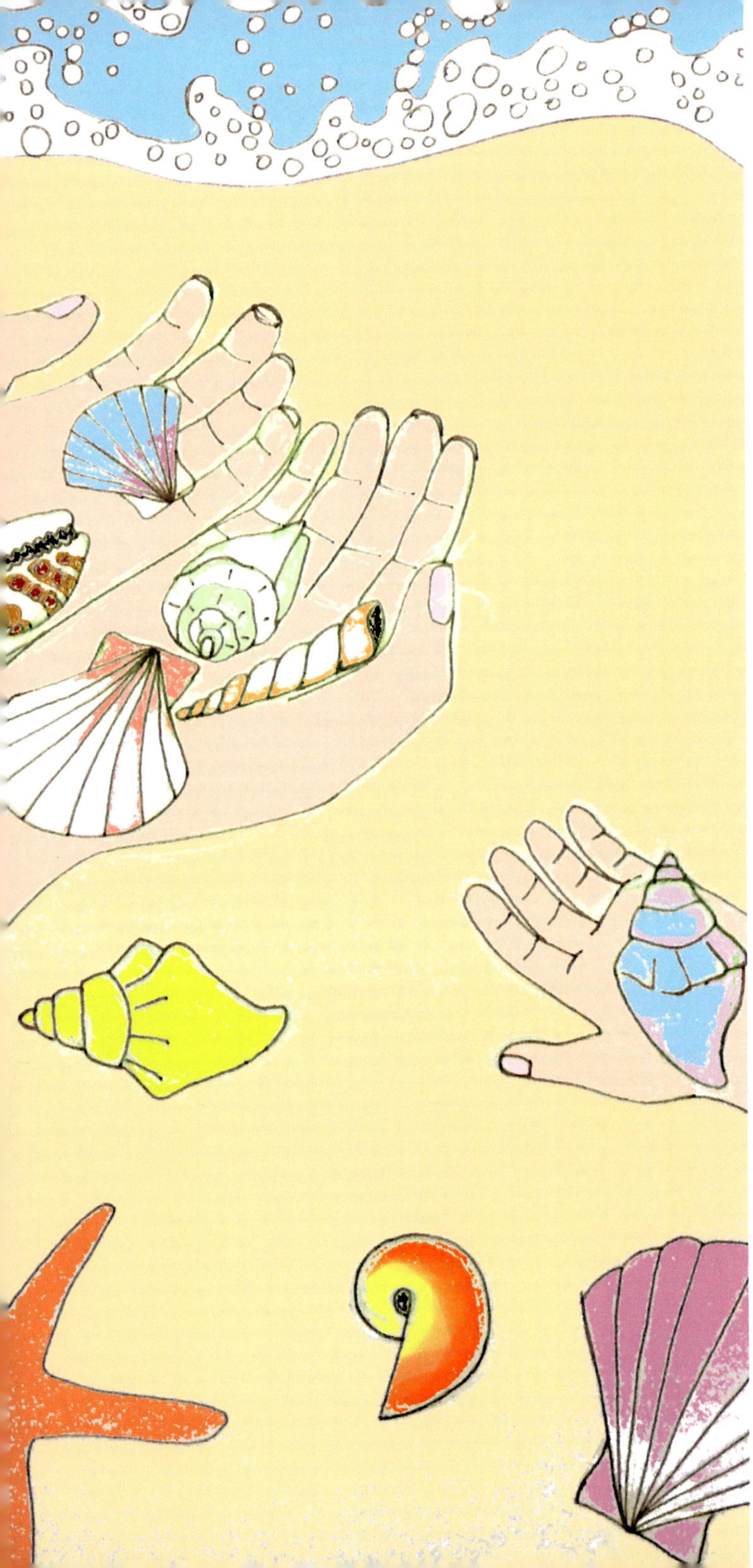

SEA-SHORE SHELLS

Look at the workmanship!
Tented limpet shell or pearly top,
Ridged or ringed in careful camouflage,
Perfect coil, or even slope.

Look at the strength!
Hands can do nothing here to crack or rip.
Only a rock, with battering, shattering force
Could smash or chip.

Think of the patience!
Quietly feeding under the sea's swell
Among the rocks and the seaweed, cropping
Material to grow this rock-like shell.

Think of the tenacity!
Huddling in crevices against the hurling sea,
The mighty pull and drag, to suck them free,
Clinging to the dull rock, against the wash and
swish.

Clamped in the cliff:
Fossils of these heroes' ancient ancestry.
Here on the beach:
Last monument to humdrum life,
This tiny legacy.

THE PEARL

When the grit gets into your being:
Not swishing through, then gone,
Not just pausing, with the tide fleeing,
Dropped in your shell, then swirling on,

Piercing your membrane, ***penetrating*** your self;
Every movement, a rip of pain;
Open or closed, on your rocky shelf,
The hurt inside you will never leave again.

No use to ignore it! The searing flash
Magnifies every motion, every urge.
Actions you hadn't noticed wake the lash
Of wounded flesh, rawness that longs to merge.

-- The suffering oyster gives its best:
Silky strength surrounds the speck,
Layer on layer, to earn some rest
And cushion the pain of that flaming fleck.

A pearl, jewel of serenity,
Wouldn't have happened without the hurt.
Dreamy peace, clouds of eternity,
Have wrapped in beauty that grain of dirt;

And when this little life has reached its end,
Peace at last, under the rocking tides,
Here is the treasure that will send
Divers searching, thrilled, where it hides.

A precious moon of loveliness lies in your hand;
No trace of the torture that bought its birth;
Silvery orb of mystery, veiling the sand
That made this life a million's worth !

FEATHERS

Feathers and flight: a double breakthrough!
Feathers or flying: which came first?
The air to conquer: develop and make new
Apparatus: new life-style to be nursed.

Flick! Flick! Flexing a quill against my thumb;
Willowy strength! Supple resistance to my push:
The lightweight strut of hollow horn,
The strands, combed perfectly, -- to ride the rush

And climb the batting air; bank and turn;
Ruler of the unseen element; every sweep
Hauling sky, reaching for space, churn
The eddying winds: home flutter or soaring leap.

A double breakthrough: feathers and flight!
Flying or feathers: which came first?
Strong and flexible, so warm and light:
Perfect comfort, perfect equipment. -- Burst

From the ground in soaring elegance;
Power and thrust ruling the sky;
Smaller cousins, in fluttering competence,
Chattering tumbles, the bushes flash by.

Back to the nest: devoted family fuss,
In trees or cliffs or mountains. Warm and soft,
The feathers defy the landscape, teaching us
Homely comfort, snug, after exploits aloft.

Feathers and flying, a double breakthrough!
Flight or feathers: which came first?
The air is conquered! And with this new
Apparatus, a whole life-style can be nursed.

Out of the Dreaming Dark 54

AIRBORNE !

Was it fear, or hunger, or just plain fun
That drove you to conquer the empty element:
Grasp along branches, head for the sun,
Glide off to safety, in repeated experiment?

Desperate refuge from the milling throng;
A step too far where the branch grows weak;
Hurtling through air, with a startled song;
Generations' adaptation of claw and beak.

Working the wind, balance and ride,
Soar and hover, serene and safe.
The sky is yours, who scuttled to hide
And reached for infinity, desperate waif!

Manoeuvre in strength, or fluttering skill;
Superb in your element; freedom on high;
Power and speed, or almost still;
Graceful rulers of trees and sky.

HIGH HOPES

When the egg breaks
And everything seems possible;
As the chick shakes
Shell-shards from sticky down;
As the world wakes,
Inviting, exciting, accessible,
And the youngster takes
First hopeful steps: a clown

In stubby down, sweet chick-chick fluff;
A darling scraggy pompom; wings no match
For all its dreams; feathers not strong enough
For the wide world; teach it to peck and scratch!

Among the debris of the cluttered nest,
Stretching with useless wings, to shake the air;
Squawking at parents: “Give me the best!
Why can't I get my own yet? It's not fair!”

Hop a few inches, while dreaming of miles;
Scold and squabble; make the gawky wings flap;
Beg and feed, while each parent smiles;
Bigger; growing beautiful; till leaping the gap

Into air! Dizzy ecstasy! Rhythm and sweep:
All that was practised on dusty ground;
No more waiting; no more tumbles; the great
longed-for leap
Into freedom, adventure, the last thrilling bound!

Now the air sings
Through the confident climb,
And the earth swings
Far from the circling feet.
The ascension brings
Panorama sublime!
On glorious wings,
Mount to the beat!

BROODING

Love sits immobile: the hen bird or the cock
Still as a statue, never a feather flutters;
In carven detail, whatever breezes rock
The dappling leaves, however the fresh wind
mutters.

Unnoticed in the landscape, patient love
Alert, daylong, motionless at its work;
Warm, loving, unmoving, it broods above
Unyielding eggs, watchful till life shall jerk.

In stillness and in faith, giving what's needed:
Warmth, and with it life, for the hidden chick.
The bright unblinking eye stares straight, unheeded;
Stillness and warmth, silence, to nurture the quick

-quick-quickening life that taps at last,
Pecking and struggling, straggly, no feather in place;
No peace, as it surges and seeks; idleness is past.
This life looks for liveliness, exploring its space;

Yet still, in danger or tiredness, gathered to rest,
Sheltering, loved, in stillness, under the warm breast.

Out of the Dreaming Dark 56

THE SINGING GARDEN

Phee-wee-oot, Tip-a-tip-tip, Coo-roo,
Phee-wee-oot, Tip-a-tip-tip, Coo-roo;
Phee-owt, Phee-owt, from the chimney-pot,
Prrr-ut, Prrr-ut, from the swing,
Twiwiwitwitwit-trr, from the bushes,
Listen to the garden sing.
Ee-phee-it, Ee-phee-it, Ayee-up, Ayee-up.
Tt-chrr, Tt-chrr, Phee, Phee.
Twirty-up, Twirty-up, Twirty-tooy, Twirty-tooy,
Chuppy-chup-chup-chup-chup, Phee, Phee.
From every corner, “Here I am.
Singing my own song, Phee-ee!
Hidden, but holding my place;
All that I am, poured out in my song.”
Phe-twee-it, Phe-twee-it, Pwp-brrr, Pwp-brrr;
Ee-aw, Ee-aw, twit-a-wit.
Trri-tri-trrr, Trri-tri-trrr, Pfee-up, Pfee-up,
Tt-t-whr-rrr, Tt-t-whr-rrr, Twit-tu;
Twitwit-tooit, Twitwit-tooit, Twee-ut, Twee-ut,
Ph-eer! Ph-eer! Pffoo-coo,
Ee-phee-it, Ee-phee-it, Coo-roo, Coo-roo,
Phetwee-eet, Phetwee-eet, Coo-roo.

THE SONG

Almost hidden among the twigs,
The thrush at his chirruping fills the air with song:
Three poplar trees, the gardens where he digs,
This bridge, the railway track: how sweet and strong

That chirruping song embraces all, lifts all,
Brings to life, with his call, and answering calls
And echoes interweaving. A concert hall
Would be no match for this patch,
Arching the garden walls.

Like the song filling the sky,
Our life and deeds spread out in harmony
Bigger than we know. Wide and high
Our call, and answering calls, in symphony,
With echoes interweaving, zig-zag the walls;

Rousing other lives; answers everywhere;
What's in our hearts sings out, to fill the air.

THE ALBINO PIGEON

The albino pigeon shuffled its feet
And drooped its snowy head.
Limp and thirsty in the show-tent's heat,
It wished that it was dead.

Around it, shades of pearly grey
And subtle pink and green
Strutted and preened the time away,
Impatient to be seen.

Fantails and perfect pouters,
Blue-greys, flashes or bars,
Parading without doubt, as
They waited for rosettes and stars.

What rosettes for a milk-white misfit,
Plain, with never a glimmer?
While every pearly outfit
Courts the light with its shimmer?

Judges compare the pearly greys
And their collars of green and pink.
Blanko is slumped in a dismal daze,
Till it jolts itself to think:

“Stand up! Stand up for simplicity,
Untouched, unmarked, unstarted!
Don't let me be charged with complicity
In my own defeat, faint-hearted!

“Folk will grow sick of the shades of grey
And every inbred shadow.
‘Glad of the brightness of white,' they'll say.
Suddenly, I'll be the fellow.”

Judges will give rosettes and stars
To the perfect greys they love,
But at last the albino pigeon
Takes the prize: for a pure white dove!

THE PIGEONS' GARLAND

Army of butlers in sober grey,
They browse across the lawns.
Sensible, quiet, no heroes they!
A grey existence, no thorns.

Quiet coo and gentle flutter,
A calm, contented throng,
Collecting crumbs from path or gutter;
Clean sweep as they stroll along.

Cooing closeness before day dawns,
Planning the parade, when tourists come.
But, Oh! The tedium of crossing the lawns!
Ceaseless patrol for every crumb.

No wonder they're grey! Yet on tourist shoulders
Gentle birds make generous friends.
Not much squabbling. Only the bolder
Perch and peck. Supply never ends.

Endless tourists and endless birds;
Endless handfuls of seed.
Endless delight! No need for words;
Relaxing smiles as they feed.

A hint of rainbow magic, seen
Among the endless grey;
Glint of pink and sheen of green
On friendly birds, whose day

Is spent in patient duty,
Back and forth across the lawns;
That shimmer of jewelled beauty
Each faithful neck adorns.

Out of the Dreaming Dark 59

BLACKBIRDS

“Here you are, son. Eat your fill!”
Says the blackbird to his chick,
And our dad, at the windowsill,
Whispers: “You lot! Come and watch! Quick!”

The big chick stands with gaping beak
Trying his best to look helpless;
Doesn't care that his father's been coming all week,
Raggeder each day, unselfish.

Blackbird stoops and prods and mimes,
Pecks the food, then drops it.
Chick does nothing. Three more times.
- Then cat walks by, and stops it.

Successful retreat to the sycamore tree,
Where other chicks sit waiting.
Cat grows tired; wanders off, to see
Are there any other sites worth baiting?

When cat's asleep, we watch again.
The lesson is soon restarted.
Still the cock blackbird, - Where's the hen?
And the chick, playing thick, to be partied.

Family, crowding the windowsill,
And blackbird share one wish:
When will the chick learn to fill his bill
Himself, at the cat-food dish?

THE PEACOCK'S PRAISE

The peacock spreads his tail, and stands,
And steps, and stands again.
The thoughtful breeze lifts a few strands
And lets them spread again:
Strands of copper and gilt,
Exquisite workmanship,
And, in another light, a sea-green glint.

The peacock turns, shrrrr-rr-rrs his fan,
And turns, still spread.
His frozen cosmos of whirling eyes,
Copper till now, floods green.
The floating silk –
Such emerald and blue, turquoise and gold –
Medieval colours, jeweller's craft.

No other prayer is needed.
Here he stands:
Perfect praise and thanks.

THE PEACOCK'S FAMILY

Through the shrubbery, drab, between dry sticks,
Dull as a dowager steps the quiet peahen.
Almost invisible, three scruffy chicks
Clamber in her wake, like fussy children.

The emperor's family, yet no regal train
Nor fanfare of outriders clears their way:
A private journey, without fuss or strain:
Among the sheltering twigs no banners sway;

But royal blood will out! Dull plumage, yet
Each peachick flaunts a shimmering coronet.

STREET PEACOCK

Like any scruffy teenager,
When first they start to roam,
The peacock on the pavement
Half a mile from home;

A ragged autumn morning:
Parked cars and slimy street;
Suddenly, this emperor's envoy
Precedes us, on dainty feet.

Turn aside to the little churchyard,
Where trees salute the cold.
Here, for your honour's pleasure,
The ground is spread with gold.

Out of the Dreaming Dark 61

ALBINO PEACOCK

You are unreal! White drift along hot wall,
Like snow among the ivy; gap in the shade;
Resting, cotton-white; the damask fall
Of trailing feathers bids the shadows fade.

Challenge to peacock glory! Negative splendour!
Blank nothing where the dazzling shades should shimmer.
No sheen or sparkle to make light your friend or
Tease the shadows with a dancing glimmer.

Just peace, just gentle white, no hassle you!
A quiet amble through the drowsy shrubs.
Our questions trail behind. Alternate view!
A blind white hole imagination stubs:

A cut-out in the path; blank vacancy;
Your bridal train of nothing drains our mind.
Pure feathered emptiness! Sheer nullity!
Our thoughts spin dizzy as we step behind.

White doves have never challenged my belief,
Nor trailed me, captive, in their fluttering track,
But here my wild surmise gets no relief:
Mesmerised, gawping at your plain white back.

DUCKS IN THE ORCHARD

September in Newby Gardens:
Autumn's golden light,
English red-and-green apples,
Fit for the young Snowhite.
Apples ferment where they've tumbled.
Cider wafts on the breeze
And the ducks are drunk in the orchard
Under the apple trees.

Soon the muddle of winter
Will turn the apples to mush.
The ducks will retreat to the rushes
When the lawns are sloppy with slush.
Wild winter is cleaning the landscape.
Branches crack in the breeze,
Where the ducks were drunk in the orchard
Under the apple trees.

Spring is a bride in her finery:
Blossom on every bough.
The drifts that spread in the orchards
Are pink and white petals now.
Flakes of apple blossom
Float on the dancing breeze,
Where the ducks were drunk in the orchard
Under the apple trees.

Summer is busy with ducklings.
Proudly the parents strut,
Or risk their brood on the river,
Or relax when the gardens are shut.
The apples are small, but growing.
They nod to the bustling breeze.

Out of the Dreaming Dark 62

Soon the ducks will be drunk in the orchard
Under the apple trees.

Another September turns golden.
The butterflies lurch and swagger.
Among the fallen apples
The ducks hobble and stagger.
Autumn has flung her bounty
And spread her riches to please
And the ducks are drunk in the orchard
Under the apple trees.

HORNBILLS

Two gossips sitting on a branch,
Bored, relaxed and lazy.
To call them models of romance
Seems distinctly crazy.

Hunched in their sooty feathers
With a megaphone each for a beak;
Crouching like commentators
Waiting their turn to speak;

Companions in beak management
With square, strong tails for balance,
Where is the graceful courtship
Of flirting, feathered romance?

Security's a problem for hornbills:
They aspire to a peaceful life,
So the doting hornbill husband
Walls up his darling wife.

Safe from the thieving monkeys
And circling birds of prey;
Proud chatelaine in her turret
Rocked by the branches' sway.

Immured for the species' safety,
Cramped, on her prison nest,
She turns the eggs over gently,
Brooding and dreaming, at rest.

Back- and forwards the hero
Flies with his gifts of fruit:
Supplies for his cherished captive.
He knows what tastes will suit.

Like Pyramus to Thisbe:
“Oh wall, show me thy chink!”
he looks for the gleaming eyeball
and feathers black as ink.

At last, when the chicks are ready
To recognise father's call,
What a hooting of hornbills!
As they all break through the wall.

Away to the leafy branches
And lazy contemplation!
Nature's old-fashioned romantics
Prosper by immuration.

GOLDEN PHEASANT

Gleaming blue, and dark green edged with black;
You dither back and forth in your airy shed;
Toting a world of colour on your back,
Pedlar's samples, shining yellow and red.

Camouflage! Oh, excellent excuse
For all this opulence of glossy plumage;
Red and blue and gold all put to use;
Black trim to every feather shapes the image.

The gilded helmet, like a pharaoh's wig
Marks regal status, matched by stately strut;
Your dainty claw, poised under gorgeous rig,
Your sweeping glance, proud eye, disdainful foot.

Do servants throng, to comb those gorgeous feathers?
Do sycophants hover, to please your every whim?
Just a dowdy wife, companion in all weathers:
Khaki and black her faithful, practical trim.

Your life no different from so many others:
Courtship, nesting, patiently pecking grain;
But nature, in flamboyant bounty, smothers
You, cherished bird, in tints for an emperor's train.

MAGPIES

Navy and white, so smart and grand,
You strut, correct and stately.
The shining blues that glow as you stand
Flash like an emperor's livery.

The spread of your stripes as you leave the ground
Is breath-taking with its pattern.
As you swoop through the trees, or circle around,
No camouflage for you! Bold villain!

Raucous clatter, painful to hear,
Your voice betrays your nature:
Traitor in evening dress! Badge of fear!
Drumming noise threatens every creature.

Few little birds in our gardens now,
And the gardeners blame the magpies,
Plundering and robbing on every bough;
Terror to all that flies.

Yet, alone, I saw you, on a speeding road
Pick your way through the traffic
To clean up a cadaver. Cars never slowed.
You stepped, level-headed, no panic.

Reliable, obstinate, back and forth
To finish the chore that's your nature:
Clean up the offal, and show us your worth:
The niche that belongs to each creature;

So, brush off your uniform. Wear it with pride!
-- Though your rattle sets my teeth on edge –
No camouflage! No need to hide!
The ‘cleansing operative' of the hedge.

MAGPIES AT A ROADSIDE CAFE

(Seen during my gap year travels)

What a beautiful photo it would have made:
The bleached tree, the magpies, the distant shade;
Three pairs flirting on the naked branches,
Distant pairs skimming, taking their chances;
Smart livery of dazzling blue and white
Catches the eye: Oh, strutting, prancing sight!

But the photo wouldn't exclude the downside:
Canteen rubbish no-one has tried to hide.
Cartons and bottles and scraps of food
Cover the field in a cardboard flood.
The strutting scavengers flash like jewels:
Brilliant life that this offal fuels.
The rubbish has brought them and keeps them fed,
Bright and bold on the field so dead.

What a beautiful photo life would make,
If only the rubbish were out of the ‘take'.

LADYBIRDS

God's only a little boy really!
That's why he made the ladybird,
Like a tiny tank, marauding freely;
Greenfly-gobbler, quite absurd.

With clockwork legs and plastic armour,
Nursery-toy colours and shape to match,
Black-spotted, red or yellow charmer;
(But stinging nerve-juice to make us scratch!)

Naturalists - (those *big* little boys!) –
Tell us the colours are thoroughly practical.
Warning to predators: this taste annoys;
And hot-spots for warm starts, thoroughly tactical.

Did you ever think you'd see a tank fly?
Scales lift from fully-adapted controls.
Under the blazing summer sky
They zoom and swarm like flying jewels.

Wham! into me or Wham! into a roseleaf;
Environmental pest-control;
The gardener's friend, the aphids' grief,
Defender of the roses: greenfly patrol.

Down at their level, we all love ladybirds,
Clustered for warmth in the new spring sun;
Back to our childhood, loving those spotted sherds.
God who made the ladybird must be a lot of fun!

THE BUTTERFLY

Spring has summoned it out of the prison,
Crawling high to dry in the sun;
Surprised to feel cramped wings widen,
Pump full of fluid, grow crisp and strong.

Dainty legs clutch a swaying stalk
While the dizzy head comes to terms
With a being totally changed: no walk-
ing round chewed leaves now; confirms

The leg-count -- six -- hardly relevant !
The delicate, strong-as-steel wings
Could transport an elephant
If built in proportion. Tough rings

Encase the thorax: cockpit, instruments,
Payload, sensors and signalroom.
A few days' flight – no documents –
To flutter in the sunshine; assume

That life was made for nectar and courtship:
Twirling dances among the flowers.
Coded perfumes call to partnership.
Scented summonses fill the hours.

Does the butterfly know, it's our symbol of glory?
Carefree beauty, at play in the sun?
The old self shrugged off; a neat allegory
For our Resurrection, to eternal Son?

(cont.d)

Forget the days of munching cabbage,
Dull camouflage of green or brown,
The helplessness of the chrysalis stage,
Exhaustion and nausea, you thought you'd drown.

Now is the ecstasy of airy freedom,
Sweet indolence in scented bowers;
Guest at the honey-pots in floral kingdom;
Basking in the sunshine, or visiting the flowers.

'Mid the extravagance of florid elegance
Ferrying fertility among the blooms;
Pollen's courier, vital grains to tell again
Colours for posterity, structure and perfumes.

Messenger of peace, nobody's enemy,
Gentle and silent, you hover and twirl;
Fluttering conductor in colour/perfume symphony,
Friend of summer, in a sunfilled world.

~~~ DAY 6 ~~~

And God said,
"Let the land produce living creatures according to their species:

tame animals, creeping things, and wild animals, species by species."

And that's what happened.

God made the wild animals according to their species,

the tame animals according to their species, and all the creepy-crawlies,

species by species.

And God gave them His approval.

Book of Genesis 1, 24-5

LAND ANIMALS

The sea, the sky, and now, dry land to fill
With life that walks or jumps or crawls or swings:

Skin, or fur, or scales,
Hooves, or claws, or nails,
Grasping paws, or waving tails:
Wherever the opportunity, life clings.

Food and fun and cuddles,
Strength, excitement, muddles,
Hunting games and happy huddles;
Courtship, family life:
All, achievement brings.

QUADRUPEDS

"Quadruped:" What does it mean?
Thunder of hooves across the plains;
Cowboy herds or cossack hordes;
Speed and freedom and flying manes.

Or, slowly through the shadows,
The sloth slung among the vines,
Hung happily in forest stillness,
Toes tight round the looping lines.

Splashing bears go scooping salmon.
Hopping rabbits fill the dusk.
Ghostly squirrels float like thistledown.
Ponderous elephant sharpens a tusk.

Kangaroo, leaping long-distance;
Tortoise in armour knows its place;
Skulking wolf or scrambling gibbon:
Different lifestyles, different pace.

Prowling low or swinging high:
Four-footed variety, from sea to sky.

THE CATERPILLAR

"Bottom of the food-chain! What do you mean?"
Complaint comes crawling out of the green.
Truly invisible, unseen in the scenery,
Juicy gobbler round juicy greenery.
"If we were the bottom, we'd have nothing to eat.
Leaves forever! Just use your feet!"
Apple or oaktree, rowan or beech,
Thousands of gobblers lunching on each.
Spring-green or silver, tooth-edged or plain,
Each has its specialist: Munch! Sun or rain.
Mouth purpose-built for endless consumption
"What else is a face for? Use your gumption!
More muscles than you, as I twizzle and loop:
Two hundred, controlling each stretch and stoop.
Of course I've a brain! With all this to keep sorted:
Feet, hook-feet and cushions, all segments co-ordinated.
We're proud of our place! Foundation position;
Unheard, unnoticed; vegetation animation!"

Out of the Dreaming Dark 69

SNAKES

Slither: does it say everything?
Encapsulate the snake experience?
Conjure up a slippery way of life?
Muscular smoothness: glide and cling,
Wind and twist, or weave a waving dance,
Or vanish through the leafmould like a knife.

In speed and silence: Gone!
And leaves a gap – but no gap! – Was it there?
Still as a photograph. No movement! None!
The eery glide vanished in thin air.

But when the chill slows the lonely slither:
Clinging closeness of the hibernating heap
In sibling comfort. Above, the leaves wither;
Contented tangle of the winter sleep.

KANGAROOS

What is the answer for a semi-arid wilderness –
Not desert! Not simple desert!
Brushwood and waterholes, scattered in the emptiness:
Reach it? How can we reach it?

A tempting train of sustenance to criss-cross the wilderness:
Islands! Like islands in the dry!
With green on the horizon, gasp across the emptiness;
But distance! A quadruped can't fly!

And so the quadruped became a cinqÜeped,
And of that cinq, uses only three:
Boing! across the empty miles; Boing! till supper; Boing! till bed;
Spacehopper laps the emptiness; spacehopper, hopping free.

Tail, like a spring, maintains the bouncing impetus;
Back legs keep the rhythm, on and on:
Old Man Kangaroo, king of the spaced-out wilderness;
Friendly family groups, seen and gone.

Out of the Dreaming Dark 70

What about youngsters in the semi-arid wilderness?
Short legs slow you down, die of thirst!
Hoist them in your pocket as you bounce across the emptiness.
Put them down, when you've covered the worst.

No dramatic patterns in the dusty, gritty wilderness:
Sandy fawn or khaki, camouflage!
Space-hoppers and their hitch-hikers fade into the emptiness.
Boing! With tails and pockets, we're in charge!

REACHING

Dawn lies golden over the grassland.
Out-stretched shadows welcome the days.
Massed in the mist of the waking land,
Animals float in the pearly haze.

Like islands, wreathed in wispy silver,
Clumps of trees reach for the sky.
Roots drink deep while water's still there.
Juicy foliage tempts on high.

Graceful giraffe and hefty elephant
Shared one problem: how to reach;
Find solutions, clumsy or elegant;
High and wide, grasp food for each.

Across the swaying, sunlit grassland,
Giraffes in patchwork, camouflage stains;
Browsing, gossiping, there they stand,
Necks erect like working cranes.

Elephant grunts as it humps and heaves,
Lumbering grey like a walking boulder;
Coiling trunk among the leaves;
Throwing the remnants over his shoulder.

Green retreats from the dry savannah.
Rains are over. Brown returns.
Herds move on, in the age-old manner.
Hot air dances. Empty noon-day burns.

Trees still proffer their deep-drunk greenness.
Animals browse in the welcome shade,
Following slowly. Waters may stream less
But nature's stratagems are still well-laid.

Trunks and necks among the branches
Extend the reach of nature's chances.

21ST CENTURY CAMEL

It's a lazy life for a camel
In the twenty-first century.
Nobody needs us for travelling
Or the journeys that used to be

But we still look good in the landscape,
Draped in a colourful rug,
And I won't even try to spit in your eye
On good days; give me a hug.

You'll look your best in your photos;
High in the saddle we'll set ya,
To rock you around the pyramids
Or canter down steps in Petra.

My cousin's a racing camel,
And rides in the back of a lorry
To races in distant places.
If he loses, they'll make him sorry.

But I just wait for tourists
And snooze in the sun all day.
And sometimes I dream of Christmas
And Jesus, asleep on the hay.

LIKE A LIZARD

Like a lizard on a rock, just basking,
Just being itself, warm in the sun's rays;
Spread out in the welcome warmth; no asking
What the day brings, after the dawn haze.

Warm on the warm rock under the sun's eye;
Warm with life, full joyful to be,
Just being, full of well-being; no worrying why
This lucky life, lazy, where the sun can see.

And life brings juicy leaves and crunchy insects,
Rocks to scuttle, and cracks to shade from the heat,
Other lizards to play with. Eye inspects
The waiting landscape; lounging still; warmth so sweet.

So we, seen and seeing, lie in love's gaze,
Enabled, empowered, soaked in sun;
Adored, adoring, drenched in sweet love's rays;
Our place to be, warming, resting. No done

Deed shall outshine the peace God offers:
Before and after and always, God's gift, to his lovers.

Jn 14, 27; 20, 20

ONE LONELY SHEEP

Sixty million sheep are jealous
Of the one that got away.
Sixty million sheep went nowhere
But Shrek went far away.

Away from the count, away from the dip,
Away from the annual shearing;
Away to the hills, away to the cliffs,
Away to a cave in a clearing.

Sixty million sheep were grazing
Safely in their farmers' care.
Just one lonely sheep was AWOL,
No-one knowing he wasn't there;

Lonely on the winter mountains,
Bleating sadly through the rain;
Heavy as a walking wool bale,
Longing to be shorn again.

Till, up from the farm, up from the fields,
Up came the farmer, searching,
And out from the cave, down from the cliffs,
Rescued his woolly foundling.

Sixty million sheep unnoticed;
Shrek gets shorn on live tv.
Sixty million nameless fleeces;
Shrek's is sold for charity.

Now, don't stray lonely on the mountains.
Don't shiver through the storm, alone.
Stick with the flock, through storm or sunshine.
Your master's glad you're safe at home.

Remember Shrek? New Zealand's only famous sheep, found 2004, RIP 2011

MOTHERHOOD

A timid tabby haunts the empty plot,
Shadow among the shadows, grey in the gloom.
The leaves hang still and chill where she is not.
Soft swish behind her shows where they made room.

Between the twilit twigs her dappled shape
Flits like a ghost, unheard, on silent paws,
Or fades along the alleys; soft escape
Matching the dimness, noiseless past the doors.

Yet, now, her half-grown kittens are shown with pride,
Installed near the railings. Passers-by can dote.
Close, in the bushes, tabby can safely hide,
Frantic, but fond, enjoy the praise, and gloat.

The opening gate brings terror to the plot.
The guardian mother towers like a ghost in the gloom;
Tigress with blazing eyes: Ah! Touch ye not!
Approach not this bristling vengeance; grey, spitting doom!

Desperate courage flares in the timid eyes.
Centuries of feline power rage in that glance.
Who can brave this gaze that petrifies?
In mid-step, frozen, the admirer halts his advance.

The intruder gone, a timid, nervous shape
Flits back to the bushes, dissolves, where shadows gape.

Out of the Dreaming Dark 74

KITTEN LOVE

Tumbling kittens, black and white,
Tails and paws in a whirling ball.
Threaten! Stand off! Take to flight!
Ricochet round the cluttered hall.

Nature practises teeth and claws:
Lunge and parry; Square for a fight;
Empty biting with silent jaws;
Pat and push and butt out of sight.

Testing each other, scares and scuffles;
Wary and watchful; giddy fright;
Silent stalking; carpet muffles
Even mistakes, as they thud from height.

Wrestling playfully, cuffs and cuddles;
Warm and brotherly, no real spite;
Glimpses of tigerhood peep through the muddles:
Strength and ferocity, skill and might.

Fondling, finding strengths and weaknesses;
Clutching and clawing, clasping tight.
"Aren't they sweet," murmur doting witnesses,
Charmed by the bonding, brotherly sight.

Patting and playful, lying together
Head to tail, they fit just right;
Tail curled softly round each brother;
Relaxation, trusting quite.

Sleeping kittens, black and white,
Curled round each other, like day and night.

DEBUTANTES

Our five-month kitten just wants to go clubbing,
With dancing paws and twirling tail, ears pricked,
Pert, pleading face and nifty whiskers; rubbing
And purring round our ankles: Don't get kicked!

We'll keep her in till she's been spayed at Christmas,
To save us from a wealth of tortoiseshell:
More pattering paws! And all that litter business!
Too young to be a mum, so guard her well!

Out teenager just wants to go out clubbing:
Proud-walking, shaven-headed, trendy gear;
Young, open heart, free spirit. Is *she* rubbing
Against the kind of friends we want *her* near?

We can't cage her, nor keep her in till Christmas
To smash her wings against the prison walls.
We must lengthen out her tether: it's the business
Of parenthood. Outside, the big world calls.

She's restless, like a boat that bobs at anchor;
Let her practise in the bay, a few more turns;
Then trust her to the ocean. If it sank her,
We'd rescue her. Let's hope that she returns!

We wish her happy ventures and safe harbour!
It's much simpler with the kitten: we'll just guard
her!

BELONGING

"Is it your cat, then? Comfy, on your doorstep?"
Steady eyes, sphinxlike, answer my gaze.
"Mangy and thin, it couldn't go one more step;
Slumped in the hall here, end of the autumn days."

Dark tabby, rippled like the ribbed sea sand:
"How could such curling comfort go unfriended?
Huddled on the sofa for a stroking hand;
Food bills and vet's bills till the winter ended."

The ball of tabby comfort makes no move,
No twinge of sadness at its own sad story:
A famished and flinching stray, looking for love,
Now purring, fat and fed, in fluffed-out glory.

"We'd miss it, though we never wanted one;
Much better here than roaming on the rubble."
-- Patterned doorstop in the evening sun, --
"It thinks it's ours now, after all our trouble."

Behind your backs, the furry heap'll
Wink one eye, quite sure *you* are *its* people.

GARDEN MYSTERIES
(Grey Squirrel)

Why two red tulips among the yellow?
And why one yellow among the red?
And why one glorious golden fellow
Lonely, in my neighbour's flowerbed?

Why the neat holes that scatter the lawn?
New chestnut sprouting under the swing?
What mischief done before the dawn
Has soundlessly rearranged everything?

Sometimes we see his feathery silver
Balance and float through the winter trees;
Or watchful still, through frosty shiver,
Grey squirrel, active despite the freeze;

Clutching a nut, like a bright-eyed statue,
But brown eyes restless, always alert;
Hop, skip, pause: still more nuts to rescue?
Leaping faultlessly over the dirt;

Endless activity, graceful, unhurried,
The ghostly gardener alters our schemes.
Collecting, digging, retrieving what's buried:
Will he open new vistas or scatter our dreams?

UNDER THE LARCH TREES

The earth is black and brown
Under the hidden sky:
Pine needles crumbling down
To layers of peat. A dry

And lifeless, soundless world
Muffles the exploring tread.
The crack of a snapping twig
Arrests us, so dry, so dead.

What is there left to thrill us
Under the homely sky,
Since Attenborough swayed with gorillas
In lazy amity?

The book of nature is read now,
Familiar from cover to cover.
We might as well stay in bed now!
There's nothing left to discover.

But something no-one has shown me
Attracts on the dreary ground:
White threads round a centre, only
A dark hole. What have I found?

Surely the lair of a spider!
In English woods! What a find!
Like frost, the wispy, hider
Circles. Over there! And behind!

The ground is black and brown,
But nature makes use of the gloom.
Just let your eyes look down:
Inventiveness has found some room.

~~~ Day 6 ~~~
(cont.d)

Then God said,
"Let us make human beings in our image,
like us, to look after the fish in the sea and
the birds in the sky, all the tame and wild
animals, and all the creatures that move
along the ground."

So God created human beings in his own
image,
in the image of God he created them;
male and female he created them.

God blessed them and said to them,
"Be fruitful and multiply; fill the earth and
look after it. You are in charge of the fish in
the sea and the birds in the sky and every
living creature that moves on the ground."

God inspected all He had made, and highly
approved of it. Evening was followed by
morning—the sixth day was complete.

Thus the heavens and the earth were
completed in all their vast array.

Book of Genesis 1,26 – 2,1

HUMAN BEINGS

God saw such rich creation
All nameless, unaware;
Beauty and power and patience,
All instinct, without care.

"Let us make conscious beings,
To be like us, creators,
Working by thoughts and feelings:
Builders, potters, writers.

"Strength and skill and heartache
To sculpt or farm or weave:
Shoes or cakes or music,
Products to sell or give.

"They'll have to learn interdependence,
Yet valuing each their own:
Progress by mutual assistance,
None could survive alone.

"Just as the sheep love their shepherd
And the baker takes pride in his bread,
The joy of the co-creators
Shall be our joy," God said.

FOUR ELEMENTS – THE BAKER

Jovial muscle-man, I wrestle and heave,
Thumping this sticky lump, - what dignity here?
Some times for action, some times to leave
In calm, let things grow, change of atmosphere.

I, too, master four elements: grain from the ground,
Ground into softness, water to mix, and life added;
Life to be worked at, to pummel and pound
And abandon, to grow on its own, doubl-, trebl-, ev'n quad-ed.

Breathe deeply, puffing to size that secret life:
A secret we can encourage but cannot create.
Earth, water and air have made us a loaf,
Now fire! The final ordeal; another hot wait.

Just boring bread, with crispy crust and soft inside,
And a tired baker, aching biceps, sweating brow;
But you will be fed, with taste you trust, and crumbs to hide:
Four elements, and life! So chew in wonder now!

FOUR ELEMENTS – THE GLASS-BLOWER

Master of all the elements, like a conductor
Weaving each music into a symphony,
You summon each power, all that it has to offer,
Mixing each magic into your mystery.

Sand, dug from the ground, turns liquid, like water;
Swirling glob in the midst of the flame;
Air, blown from your mouth, will shape it, to order;
New-captured bubbles, stored on their racks, all the same.

Transparent as water, glass swells like a shell in protection,
Clean and clear, displaying its contents with gleam;
Inviting us into its lightscape, with mirroring reflection,
Worlds in miniature, wandering lights' icy beam.

Spirits of air and water, fire and earth,
Tethered, by craftsman's precision, in glittering girth.

PLATO & Co

Worlds within worlds: the old philosophers!
Little they knew, of glass to magnify,
Scrutinise, identify, sort, label, tame the fuzz
Of swirling atoms teeming, too small for eye.

Yet in their minds they hold reality,
Ponder the real and formulate Ideal:
How potter's plan achieves solidity;
Engraver focuses to carve a seal;

So minds engage to vision world in world,
And worlds beyond, flung outward, flowering
Forever, filling the void, in layers swirled
And inward; seek the core; gaze lowering.

Did they seek the Mind behind it all?
When they had cleared the shelf of pagan gods,
Grasped their futility, seen Zeus fall;
Summoned still to probe beyond the odds?

Out of the Dreaming Dark 81

NOAH'S PEACOCK

(Mosaics in St Mark's basilica, Venice)

The look on Noah's face says it all,
With the peacock's tail under his arm:
How to get this creature through this porthole
And keep its lovely plumage safe from harm?

We stand in the twentieth century
And marvel at the medieval draughtsmanship,
But most of all we love the sense of humour
That brought such understanding to his craftsmanship.

Accepting the constraints of the building,
The artist has mapped out a wall of glory,
Not skimping on the fiddling and filling;
Mosaic celebration of the ancient story.

The other birds are chatting together,
Waiting quietly in pairs or in sevens;
Such detail of beak and feather;
All the commonalty of the lakes and of the heavens.

There strut the cockerels, in a group with speckled hens,
Behind them, many a goose and gander;
Harmonious domesticity; no straying, although no pens
Have fenced them here; content, too tame to wander.

A gorgeous pheasant and his pretty, speckled wife
Stand aside for Noah, by the door;
Partridges and gamebirds and much of water-life,
Teal and mallard, as though resting by the shore.

The centuries dissolve that came between us.
We share in Noah's dilemma:
How to do the job that's been given us
Without damaging a single feather!

The magpies are squawking: "What's the hold-up?
Did they ***have*** *to be the first in the queue?*
We can't wait until he moults. You've made him fold up.
Get ***on*** *with it! You'll easily get him through!"*

Noah listened to God, and was willing
To build the enormous ark: Sure, no trouble!
But the challenge comes when you start filling
In the details: Get this peacock through this porthole!

By the time the sons arrive, each queuing with his wife,
Noah's task is almost complete.
He's loading the eagles, and the last of water-life:
Pelicans and cranes and storks, with dainty-stepping feet.

And we take good cheer from the craftsman
Who shaped his scene to its space,
To share with us the beauty of creation,
And who knew, a sense of humour has its place.

THE SPARK - MICHELANGELO'S ADAM

'*Yoo-oo-ou touch my finger tips . . .*' just nearly,
And the spark leaps, that kindles my being.
Me! Loved! Transformed! So clearly
Myself! Step taller, seeing

A self that steps out into fullness
Like the chick emerges from its shell;
No constraints or shackling dullness.
Your gaze confirms. Let my confidence swell.

So the real self catches the spark of love,
The glowing life that warms us into action.
Michelangelo's Adam reaches for Jehov-
Ah: the thrill: love's blessing: affirmation

Of all we are, yet more! Blessed into being
A greater self, more real; our full potential
Not fully grasped, but welcome; still freeing
From wispy mists that draped the essential.

Two hundred years before the scientists
The artist used the flicker of life's spark
To animate that creative moment;
So, in the eyes of love, like breathless artists,
We glimpse a self, new-summoned from the dark,
To tame life's challenges, and grow with life's
movement.

BENJAMIN FRANKLIN : THE UNKNOWN

How many times did you fling your kite
Into the teeth of the storm?
How many months had you waited each night,
Hoping the clouds would come?

And when the kite lifted at last
And rain dripped down the string,
How sure were you, as the moments passed
And you waited for the sting?

Reaching into the darkness
For power you didn't understand;
Unaware of human weakness,
Expectant, with your waiting hand;

Waiting for the spark that thrilled you,
As it jumped from the dangling key.
Did you know, it might have killed you?
Charmed life you led, scot-free!

Did you become more wary,
When you learnt of others' death?
Did your own escape seem scary,
Waiting, with baited breath?

Expectations a-prickle, poised, on tenterhooks;
Daring; fascination; not just science read in books!

PEOPLE OF PRAYER (Contemplatives)

Servants of the invisible, faithfully standing
Where people have stood for centuries:
Water from the rock, for a world demanding
Signs and wonders, comfort in life's miseries;

The all-day burdens that crush and finish
Hearts wounded and empty, with nowhere to go.
You face the God whom time can't diminish,
Who stepped right into our cares and woe;

Praising the God of all creation,
And praising him crucified, stripped of his power,
Enduring futility; the quiet resurrection
Each day, in his followers, his finest hour;

No sizzling triumph, to blast the heavens;
No enemies flung to their knees in despair;
Just quiet love, that spreads, and leavens
Life's hardships; Love learnt from God, through
prayer.

ELECTRICIANS

Servants of something invisible, faithfully following
Tables and charts and diagrams, practical and ugly;
Laying and checking cables; switches, allowing
Safe choices; twisting and tightening snugly.

No gleam of excitement in your patient work,
Careful and methodical, following the rules;
Selecting the coded colours. Here errors lurk,
Invisible too: mistakes that would trap the fools.

Success marked only by quiet pride
In machines that work, lights lit, industry humming;
Launderette, hospital, fairground ride;
Invisible power at work, doubt overcoming.

Mistakes would flare and flame, blast and dazzle,
Kill and maim under the sky;
Seering overload, with flash and sizzle
Jumping the wrong gaps; sparks or thunderbolts fly.

Invisible power shows only in results:
Baking or welding, drilling, "son et lumiere,"
Music of many kinds. Thoughtful adults,
Quietly faithful, channel the power, with care.

PYLONS

Nothing natural about a pylon!
Geometric shapes in lifeless grey;
Straight lines, sharp angles; single file on
Rolling, rounded landscape – alien way!

Giant rigid shapes ignore the contours;
Drooping wires the only gentler sign;
Graveyard hum around their silent structures;
Meaningless intruders strutting a meaningless line.

Yet! Warmth and happiness, music and light,
Hospital care and smells of warm bread,
Breweries, steel glowing, forges by night,
Cows being milked and chocolate being made

All flood through the swooping cables, strung aloft,
Aloof, seeming so sterile, steely and still;
No hint of the flowing energy; stern, nothing soft;
Only a petrified whimper, from hill to hill.

TREES

Nature's pylons: no grey silent grimness:
Graceful greenery harvests the sun;
Birds and insects in the dimness;
Bustling community; secret, chirruping fun.

Leaves rustling against the sky
Murmur a babbling lullaby to the breeze;
Or rattling under the gale, whistling *Why*
This threshing and pounding, tugging and stripping the trees?

Every species its pattern: shape of leaf
Distinctive; ripple of bark; branches arrayed,
Typical, each, of its family; true to their brief;
Gracing every landscape with shape and shade.

Tranquillity, majesty, variety adapted to the climate:
Forests of pine, or jungle of a thousand species;
Nature's powerhouses throughout the planet;
Blossom and birdsong and leafdance in the breeze.

Changing colours parade the seasons:
Gaudy autumn, naked winter, fresh new spring.
Birds seek their shelter for many reasons:
Nesting-time, berry-time, anytime to sing.

Moving shadows measure the day's length,
Golden evening through forest tunnels;
Nature's way to gather the sun's strength:
Power our planet by growing solar panels.

THE PLANT BREEDER

Hither and thither, with your instrument poised,
You dither among the flowers, like a butterfly,
Transferring pollen to the bloom of your choice.
You pause for a moment. No breeze ruffles by.

The best of the past, invisible future,
You carry your hopes at the tip of a brush;
Mating and marrying, working with nature,
Waiting and worrying: nature won't rush!

In the still greenhouse, or sealed in a bubble,
Promises of change: sweeter scent, stronger stems;
Nature enhanced. In this peace, sealed from trouble,
Successive generations yield colours like gems.

In love with the future, yet loving what's past;
At work with reality, but led by a vision;
Backing the winners, labelled and classed;
Watching out for good losers -- some rogues win remission!

Aztec dahlias, roses from Damascus,
Indian corn and Chinese chrysanths:
Patient partnership: enthuse and enrich us;
Centuries of experts, generations of plants.

THE GARDENER

As you spoke, I saw what you saw –
Your words unfolding gardens in my mind;
That still March morning, bright and raw,
Bare soil in front of us, last year's seed-heads, behind.

As you waved your arms, the scene took shape:
Your sweeping gesture drew the sweep of shrubs,
The slope of lawn. Edges, like hunger, gape,
Greedy for colour, bedding plants, bold tubs.

A splash of drama focuses the eye.
Gentler vistas invite the wandering gaze.
I saw the flowers you planned, and felt the dry
Warmth of a low wall, with scents to raise.

And as you spoke, I saw what you could not see:
Erect shoulders and sparkling eyes:
Strength to govern your kingdom; tame the free
Unloved tangle, cherish and tend and prize:

A woman who has found her metier, giving a boost
To life and nature. Here all our ambitions can roost.

Out of the Dreaming Dark 86

TAPESTRY

Translate the cottage-garden into cross-stitch
With patient in and out and to and fro.
Create design from nature. Make it rich:
Nostalgia, comfort, shapes that people know.

Pansies and hollyhocks beside the gate,
Roses or morning-glory round the door;
Honeysuckle too subtle! That must wait
Its own, more detailed, portrait. Now, ignore!

As the designer thinks of woof and weft
And marks graph-paper, smooth under her hands,
Musing the flowers she's chosen, flowers she's left,
Building a balanced scene, she understands

Her pretty cross-stitch cannot convey the reality
Of softness, dampness, vigour, growth and scent.
A little of shape and colour, square-coded beauty
Rests on her page, symbols of what she meant.

Needle and thread will prick and pull, to fill
Her canvas, with a glimpse of what she knows.
Others can share the product of her skill:
Admire the flowering love the picture shows;

Yet, honesty will catch her empty-handed:
How little is captured here of what she saw,
Still flowering in her mind; achievement blended
With impotence: such wealth! so poor a store!

Pencil and paper, just like needle and thread,
Struggle to match the beauty that we see.
Crafting God's love, the poet shakes her head,
Wordless before such bliss, all given! All free!

To JANE ASHER,

Actress, Mum, Party Cake and Costume Designer

Out of the drudgery of clothes and meals
A zingy redhead steals to teach us magic;
Fun to banish the boredom. Hear the squeals
And giggling peals! No room for anything tragic.

Three hundred and humdrum sixty days of chores,
– Relentless up and down of family life, --
Gathers momentum, rolls up its sleeves, and soars
Into overdrive, meteoric with scissors and knife.

Fabric silts up the dining-room floor.
Snippings drift from new-dreamt creation.
Out of the chaos, the sewing-machine's roar
Fanfares the frolics of a fantasy nation.

Dance away the doom and gloom
In whoo-oo-ooing fancy dress.
Mermaids shimmer and dragons fume.
Grinning broomsticks sweep through the mess.

Humpty on his wall, still ready to fall:
Boy Blue calls for his wandering flocks:
Parading picnics and stumps and ball,
Christmas parcels and fairy frocks.

Fairy-tale castles take shape out of sugar,
Sheer stuff of fantasy, goal of our dreams;
Sleeping princesses, forgetful of danger;
Sugar witch – to be eaten! – excited screams.

(cont.d)

The world of motherhood, the endless round
Of care for careless family, has annual explosion
Blasting the boredom: new energy found
In honour of the birthday. Love, the magic potion,

Keeps mother on her toes, in frantic creativity:
Twenty-hour days, to sew and bake:
Celebrate each cherished child, in annual festivity:
The loving task of motherhood; the icing on the cake!

Back at the kitchen sink, the happy glow
All champions know: success at something frivolous
Through revelry and fantasy and hectic hard work can show
The love that lights the drudgery and makes the whole year marvellous!

OFFICE BIRTHDAY

How odd, that cakes can change the focus!

Along the endless corridors,
Among the piles of patient paper,
Hands pause.
Eyes lift. A smile appears.
The automata grow real again
And step from behind their desks.
Shoulders relax. Spines flood with gentle life.
Grateful fingers reach for a fondant fancy.
Lips remember the name:
‘So, it's your birthday.
Congratulations! Doing anything special?'

Room by room, the emptying plate
Disrupts the patterns chained in paper:
A magnet attracting humanity.

One day each year, each one is special:
A few moments' attention,
Proffering festivity, on a plate;

And through the year
Each tiny spark of recognition
Warms the paperwork,
Oils the relentless systems,
And, ever so gently,
Smooths the flow.

To ALISON HARGREAVES, Mountaineer

You reached your peak, and you were first
To breathe unhampered in the icy wind
On the world's roof; sunshine's dazzling burst;
Diamond glitter of snowfields left behind.

All this is yours: the mountain walls you traversed,
The glaciers and the gulleys, marked by your axe;
Comradeship, decisions, ambitions you had nursed
And dreamed and planned: triumphant climber's climax!

Oh, Alison! There are mountains to be climbed
In our own living rooms; ridges to be scaled
Inch by inch, with stubborn dedication.
Heroine wives and mothers, not acclaimed,
Through family challenges, where others failed,
Have persevered 'cross glaciers, moved by compassion.

The icy waters of the mountain torrent
Are not as numbing as the marriage-bed
When love is frozen, and the bitter comment
Chills like the biting wind whose word's unsaid.

Just to keep moving in that frozen world;
To survive without oxygen on those glaring peaks;
Be a source of comfort and warmth, through venom hurled:
Daily domestic conquest, of which no-one speaks.

Out of the Dreaming Dark 89

What draws us onward through the rocks and mist?
For all that pain and effort, what reward?
– Learnt skills and strength and joy of sheer survival!
The sky invites to heights infinity kissed;
The blue of heaven welcomes our arrival;
The sun our fanfare, here, where light is lord!

THE PROSPECTOR

A fortune beckons beyond those hills,
Copper, uranium, diamonds or gold
Just waiting to be found. Ambition thrills
My eager thoughts: just what might the landscape hold?

Determined to fill my pack with envied treasure,
To win the praise of crowds, a bulging bank account,
To be the greatest: power the world can measure;
Untouchable, deified by wealth's amount.

The plain stretches before me, empty and bare,
Featureless and boring. why should I pay it heed?
My only purpose here is to find the rare
Tricks that will track the treasure, fulfil my greed.

Fruitless days and fretting nights,
Probing, sifting, tapping, lonely and sore,
Frustrated and obstinate, trying new sites,
Still as unyielding, but still: just one more!

Stuck in a cleft, elbows and knees bracing:
Scrabbling fingernails claw for a hold;
Or lost in the heat, light-headed, with pulse racing;
Water more precious than diamonds or gold.

Years of tracing and tracking through this vast expanse,
Grateful for shade, for a gentler slope downhill;
Grateful for water, dazzled by the glaring dance
Of heat above the rocks, but wandering still;

Growing to love the pageantry of sunset,
Birds that sing through the loneliness before dawn,
Rare flowers that surprise, in sheltered secret,
Showing me water, guarded by desert thorn.

The plain stretches before me, a well-known friend.
I've trodden every slope, jumped every crack in the rocks:
The change from sand to pebbles, the ridge's end,
The secret pools, to bathe and forget the knocks.

That's not what I came for. I've learnt to pay it heed:
The ripple of ground that tells of a change in the strata;
The shift of the dust that confides here's the water I need;
The change in the sky; rare thunderstorm following after.

A heedless adventurer came here, caring for nothing.
Now I can read the land's history, stored in the rocks,
Knowing its unique variety, valuing everything,
Slopes I have panted up, rested on pre-Cambrian blocks.

The land is my friend. Why should I sell its secrets?
The seams of coal I've found, the trickles of gold.
My wealth is peace, and the endless, bannered sunsets.
The opals that kick in my path will never be sold.

I survey my kingdom, the empty land that has taught me
My strength, taught me patience, wisdom and hope.
We belong to each other. What else could have bought me
Myself? And my sunsets? And my spirit's full scope?

THE CARTOGRAPHER

Does the landscape swell before you
As your pencil threads the lines?
Do you visit each church and windmill
As you stamp the appropriate signs?

Out of breath where the contours cluster,
Strolling where they spread wide,
Coughing in quarries' dust, or
Watching out for high tide?

Or is it the magic of symbols,
The secret music of maths,
That keeps you entranced at your tables
Until you've plotted the paths?

Yet -- ! Burning with mystic knowledge,
As you chew at your pencil stub,
Is ‘PH' the best you can manage
For all the joys of the pub?

Out of the Dreaming Dark 92

BETWEEN THE TIDES – THE FOSSIL HUNTER

My greatest enemy! My greatest ally!
Strong swing of the sea, retreating behind me:
You leave me the cliff. Demented, the gulls cry
Not to forget your rushing return will find me.

Behind my back you grumble as I work:
The ceaseless crash and rush of your forced retreat,
Distant and gentler now; and yet you lurk,
Lulling my watchfulness, longing to splash my feet.

Six hours to reconnoitre, probe and pry:
What can you show me? What have you scoured loose?
What can I rescue? Carry off safe to the dry
Desks of academe, to study the role, the use?

Both, prising the fossils from the cliff:
Yours, to continue the sculpting erosion of time;
Mine, to prise and to prize, to harvest the brief
Exposure, snatch, treasure, map history of time.

And time is against me! I glimpse you over my shoulder:
Your sneaking advance: swift swell in the quiet pools;
Wild foray foams round a jutting boulder,
Still straining to reach me. Not yet! The ebb still rules!

Often I need your help. The stubborn rock
That will not yield a fossil that I prise
And dig and chip to free, swept by the shock
Of hungry waves, will shed it, for my eyes,

Unless you steal it first, leave me empty-handed;
Or, worse! One quiet day, me forgetting my troubles,
Your silent swell encircles, grasps me, stranded:
Choking, sea-green defeat; a swirl of bubbles;

Tossed among the fossils, you strip and plunder me.
My greatest ally! My greatest enemy!

BOB GELDOF
BAND-AID, LIVE-AID

Silhouettes against a dried-out landscape,
Blue-black figures and the dusty hills,
Doom-laden commentary onto our screens:
Half a world from those scenes
Hearts are wrenched. Reaction spills
Into action: “We must find the means!”

Ever-dishevelled troubadour,
Half-broken hero,
Galvanised by those pictures of starvation,
You sang to every nation.
With lives and hope at zero,
You conjured all our hearts, to win a donation.

All our shambling hopes
Gather to the scarecrow's call,
All with their songs to sing,
With talents and hopes to bring.
The concern that binds them all
Blends harmony in the concert hall.

Can we stuff the world's problems into the OUT tray,
Processed, and tidied, and labelled “COMPLETE,”
And all lie back and sing our song:
Or must we follow him down the street,
--The dishevelled scarecrow, with the dancing feet –
Muddled, and weary, and “Why does the tune last so long . . .?”

AID WORKER ?

"We don't want to put anyone on the ground
In such a volatile situation.
Some local agents must be found;
External personnel's just an extra complication.

"Getting our own people killed
Would only make things worse.
Our objectives will be better fulfilled
By a hands-off approach: open purse." [1]

Yet God sent his only Son
Into our volatile situation.
God knows hearts can't be won
By avoiding complication;

And many of his people will be killed
To give life to local agents;
And, in giving, their hearts will be filled:
Triumph of faithful servants.

The only aid that's real:
The only aid that matters:
Is the daring gift of self
Crucified, for a world in tatters.

1 Words in italics from an aid organiser during the Rwanda crisis

To Shakespeare -
Thanks for 'ROMEO & JULIET'

And did you grieve
For strutting Elizabethans' young lives wasted?
Deaths that leave
Our hearts robbed, bitter for life half-tasted:

The gaps unfilled
For sparkling Mercutio and rash young Tybalt.
Fiery nothings spilled
Easy young blood. Now the world limps, crippled.

Grief that won't sleep:
Black boulder filling the heart's pool:
Silver rings keep
Restless watch around it. Nothing can cool

The fevered night,
Nor dissolve the bitter lump that poisons our days.
Frustrations fight
And grapple to find a meaning, peace through the maze.

You carved a jewel:
Testament to youth with all its flames,
And from that cruel
Sacrifice and heart-break, two young names

Blaze to the universe
Love's tenderness and sweet, sweet power;
Wit and agony framed in verse;
Ecstasy and deadly hour.

You plant a hope
That, though despair has stripped our hearts' bare field,
The memory of wasted love will yield
A spur, to cope.

From Homer to Kipling - MAKING SENSE

Singers of comradeship and courage,
Self-knowledge, self-mastery through the struggle,
Teamwork, discipline in the scrummage,
Leadership, loyalty, through triumph or bungle.

Seers, seeing clearly, standing aloof,
Or sharing a drink and yarns, when the crisis is over,
Seeing, amid the turmoil, lasting truth
Of daring or caring for one another.

Lying, like gems in a lava-flow,
Treasures of human growth: courage, speed,
Kindness, initiative, endurance; we owe
To times of pressure, in response to need.

And you, the seers, seeing the glint
And flicker of lasting worth amid the pain,
Sing us the music of shared effort; a hint
Of the fire that forges the steel; the gain

Whose price is bereavement and grief;
The wisdom hard-won, the kindness determined to mend;
To work despite anguish, to labour for others' relief.
You still sing the splendour of spirit that shines to the end.

POETRY SLAM York'11

All the usual suspects
Are gathered here tonight,
Wizards round a cauldron:
Let's taste if the brew is right.

All the usual suspects
Will speak their spell today:
Declaim or rant or whisper
Whatever they wish to say.

Like gold-fish in a fish-tank
Each circles into view.
Flickering fin and simpering grin:
"Now how can I please you?"

The mesmerising circling
Of silver, gold and black;
Each fish in turn at the forefront,
Then retiring, ceaseless, back.

The fishy eyes are pleading;
The fishy mouths gape wide:
"Say I'm the best you've heard tonight!
Send me home with pride."

Each one is a shining beauty,
With spots or splashes, unique.
Each one is a tireless pilgrim,
Like us, in the truth we speak.

Out of the Dreaming Dark 97

CIGARETTES –
EX-TEACHER TO EX-STUDENT

"So the life-skills classes weren't much use?"
I handed him the pack of twenty;
(Coffin-nails; you can't buy them loose)
"Sure, miss, you taught us plenty:

"Warned us of all that would shorten our lives,
So, since I've no reason to live it,
I'm grateful for all that excellent advice;
To shorten the aggro: just leave it!"

Is that all you know of life, lost in the mob,
The black weight of teenage dilemmas?
When no-one can tell you: "Yes, you're worth a job;"
So by a quick exit, you'll damn us?

The twisted smile that shows your pain;
The cheery, "I'm no use."
What can teach you that you're a gain
When you've no openings to choose?

Stick around, Please! Somebody needs you:
Your wounded wit; your twisted smile;
Scary clothes, that insist the world heeds you:
"Keep out of my way. I've got style!"

Life-skills classes and P.S.E:
We try to block off the exits,
But how can the adult world help you see
You're not just a bunch of misfits?

Each is unique in talents and skills.
Your own life must teach you your value.
The gaps will beg, till each of you fills
That space where achievement will thrill you.

Adult world, where have we failed?
Don't just teach them, "Beware of the exits."
Teach them: "Life's worth it. Don't waste it, curtailed
By packs of twenty lethal fixes."

THE PHYSIOTHERAPIST

My own physio's back today
And I can feel it;
Pulled and pummelled every way:
Will aching heal it?

The others do their best.
They have a gentler touch.
Her absence was a rest.
They didn't hurt so much.

They know they ought to be tougher.
They know it's their job;
But they don't like to see me suffer:
Hear a stifled sob.

She knows that I can do it.
She's hard as nails.
Her strength will force me through it.
She never fails.

Her faith in me
Is the power that drives her:
Hard work, to set me free,
So my pain forgives her.

Out of the Dreaming Dark 98

THE BEST ROOFER

The man who mends my gutters
Has only one good eye.
He doesn’t lose perspective
When working in the sky.

His stare is like a pirate,
Open, honest, frank.
“D’you trust him?” asked my brother.
“I’d make him walk the plank.”

His timing’s close on perfect:
I’ve noticed it before.
Whenever a job needs doing
He’ll come knocking on my door.

He notices the details.
He gives the finishing touch
And when it comes to pricing
He doesn’t ask too much.

His youngest son works with him.
They make a perfect team.
“Yes Dad,” his only comment.
They partner like a dream.

Around my neighbours’ rooftops
Other roofers swear and sway.
I’ll choose my one-eyed roofer
Over that lot, any day.